REGULATING EDEN
The Nature of Order in North American Parks

State and provincial parks are represented as inherently natural places set apart from the demands of everyday life, places that are intrinsically 'wild' and that must be protected. Yet, in order to experience the naturalness and freedom of the parks, we must embrace the very forms of regulation that we associate with places we consider to be artificial, restrictive, and alienating.

Drawing on a wide range of documents used to govern park jurisdictions, Joseph Hermer explores the character and consequences of the contradiction posed by the 'regulated Eden' of park destinations. Central to his analysis of parks as historically specific sites of governance is the notion of 'emparkment,' the practices and discourses that manufacture wildness and nature through specific forms of spatial and temporal regulation.

Using theoretical literature from the sociology of law and cultural geography, Hermer argues that emparkment order is driven primarily through discourses of both personal and environmental risk and results in an interdependency that generates powerful moralizing effects. He suggests that the mode of power constituted by emparkment is a mirror not only of how nature is configured in an era of environmental toxification, but also of how the experience of freedom itself is constructed in a society frequently characterized as repressive. Challenging us to rethink the place we have given to 'nature' in the protection of ecologically valuable landscapes, Hermer also urges us to consider the forms by which we govern ourselves in the moral order of daily life.

JOE HERMER is a post-doctoral fellow in criminology at the Centre of Criminology, University of Toronto.

Regulating Eden

The Nature of Order in
North American Parks

JOE HERMER

UNIVERSITY OF TORONTO PRESS
Toronto Buffalo London

ISBN 0-8020-4358-5 (cloth)
ISBN 0-8020-8182-7 (paper)

Printed on acid-free paper

National Library of Canada Cataloguing in Publication Data

Hermer, Joe, 1967–
  Regulating Eden : the nature of order in North American parks

  Includes bibliographical references and index.
  ISBN 0-8020-4358-5 (bound).   ISBN 0-8020-8182-7 (pbk.)

  1. Parks – Law and legislation – Canada.   2. Parks – Law and
  legislation – United States.   3. Parks – Canada – Management.
  4. Parks – United States – Management.   5. Parks – Social
  aspects – Canada.   6. Parks – Social aspects – United States.
  I. Title

  KE5207.H47 2002   346.7104′6783   C2001-902770-2

This book has been published with the help of a grant from the Humanities
and Social Sciences Federation of Canada, using funds provided by the
Social Sciences and Humanities Research Council of Canada.

The University of Toronto Press acknowledges the financial assistance
to its publishing program of the Canada Council for the Arts and the
Ontario Arts Council.

University of Toronto Press acknowledges the financial support for its
publishing activities of the Government of Canada through the Book
Publishing Industry Development Program (BPIDP).

For The Woodman

Contents

Illustrations

Preface

The experience of visiting a park holds a privileged place in our childhood memories. It is rare to find a person who does not recall childhood adventures at summer camp or on a family camping trip, or afternoons spent at a secret spot in a neighbourhood park. Remembrances of parks and parklike places survive as archetypes of innocence, places where we can somehow orient ourselves in an often alienating 'grown-up' world.

My childhood was an experience of parks in the extreme: my father is a forester, and my summers were spent working with him in a variety of park spaces. The most memorable of these summers was spent in a provincial park where we sold bundled firewood to campers from within a fenced woodyard. Cutting and bundling firewood in the summer heat was back-breaking work, and my father did not appreciate the picky comments of many of the campers, who complained that the firewood had too much bark or was too dry or too wet.

My father is a small, wiry man who does not waste many words expressing himself, and he often had a hard time holding his tongue when a camper said something especially provoking. On one occasion a man came in and picked, piece by piece, through the woodpile, until my father asked if he needed help. 'Do you have any wood without knots?' the man asked, annoyed at the apparent inconvenience. 'Wood without knots?' my father asked, rubbing his callused hands. 'You know, knots! knots!' the man said, sarcastically, holding out a piece of spruce as if my father had never seen firewood before. My father was silent for a moment. 'If we had wood without knots,' he said, motioning overhead to the shade tree they stood under, 'where would all the little birds sit?'

This book reflects on the meaning of the camper's search for a knotless version of nature, and considers the consequences of the notion of nature hinted at in my father's answer. Certainly, the image of the camper searching for a piece of knotless wood is one I often thought about years later, when I worked as a park warden, where much of my time was spent in regulatory dramas inevitably related to notions of nature and order very similar to the one held by the woodyard customer.

My approach involves examining how parks in Canada and the United States are constructed, through moral regulation, as 'official' sites of nature. This regulation helps to construct not only our notion of nature in an era of environmental destruction, but also shapes and informs our experience of freedom.

Despite my extensive critique of the contradictions inherent in government park-making projects, I would caution readers not to read between the lines an argument that celebrates the failure of the ideal of public 'emparkment.' This book was being completed just as the Conservative government of Premier Mike Harris, much to my dismay, had begun to privatize the Ontario provincial park system, a move which will only exacerbate the ways in which 'emparked' nature is complicit with widespread practices of environmental toxification. In this sociopolitical context, this book is as much a condemnation of such short-sighted political mentalities as it is an examination of the role that parks play in manufacturing the moral order of everyday experience.

Acknowledgments

This book is a revised version of my MA thesis, which I defended in the Sociology Department at Carleton University in Ottawa in the summer of 1996 under the supervision of Bruce Curtis and Alan Hunt. It is my pleasure to have the opportunity to thank them in this form for their support and friendship. The original encouragement for this project emerged from the wonderfully vibrant seminars I attended as an undergraduate at King's College, University of Western Ontario, with Joe Lella, David MacGregor, and Lesley Harman. In particular, my seminar with Joe on biography and qualitative research methods gave me the confidence to take seriously my own observations about the nature of parks and the role they play in our everyday lives.

My thanks as well to Virgil Duff of the University of Toronto Press for his patience in seeing this slim book to publication.

REGULATING EDEN
The Nature of Order in North American Parks

CHAPTER ONE

The Emparkment of Nature

The famous American conservationist John Muir's comment of a century ago, that the wildness of parks is a necessity for the 'thousands of tired, nerve shaken, over civilized people,' has never seemed more prophetic (Nash 1973:140). As places that offer us shelter from the dehumanizing surfaces of the concrete jungle, parks have come to play a crucial role in the therapy of the modern self. Our desperation to experience nature appears to be exceeded only by our ability to create equally desperate landscapes that cater to a wide range of recreational whims. Thus, we should not be surprised to read the claim that

> Even the most discerning outdoor enthusiasts and history buffs will discover the enchantment of New Mexico's 37 state parks ... There are large reservoir parks for every imaginable water sport, quiet mountain parks for hiking and camping ... a land of hidden lakes, quiet streams, and rushing rivers. Cool green forests and meadows laden with wildflowers beckon hikers, campers, naturalists and photographers. (New Mexico B)

This image from a brochure represents what we have come to expect of a park: peace, permissiveness, a space we may explore at our leisure, where nature beckons us to experience an enchanted landscape. The park destination is depicted as a primitive playland, an Eden-like garden that has been mapped and fenced off for the rejuvenation of a 'fallen' humanity lost in the alienation of modern life. Consider, however, the regulations that govern this escape into nature:

> Picnicking is allowed in designated areas from 6:00 a.m. to 9:00 p.m. or as posted. An entrance fee is charged for picnicking. Any use of a Park between 9:00 p.m. and 6:00 a.m. is considered overnight camping. Camping is allowed only in designated areas, and a camping permit is required. Overnight campsites must be vacated by 2:00 p.m. on the following day to avoid additional fee payments. Camping is limited to 14 days during any 20 day period. Camps must not be left vacant for more than 24 hours. Camp and picnic areas must be kept clean and sanitary at all times. Property left unattended for more then 14 days will be considered abandoned. (New Mexico A)

The regulation required to order this natural space presents us with a vivid paradox: in order to experience the wildness of parks, we must embrace the very forms of order and regulation we so deeply associate with places we consider to be artificial, restrictive, and alienating. Yet, this paradox is generated by a political reality: if landscapes deemed to be natural are to be protected they must be *emparked* – that is, enclosed under the protection of legislation and managed within a detailed juridical framework – a practice most commonly illustrated by the incongruent presence of regulatory signage in parks. In other words, the 'no littering' sign acts to protect nature in a form that offends the ideal of the 'natural.' It seems, then, that to 'regulate wilderness' is to preserve 'nature' by means that are antithetical to the *idea* of wilderness and those qualities that we associate with the natural. As Roderick Nash (1973) notes, the quality of freedom we so desperately look for in the wildness of parks is destroyed by intensive regulation, which turns parks into little more than 'sleeping bag motels.'

I view this paradox as one of the most significant contradictions of everyday life, one that can be explored by investigating how park destinations are 'made up' as wild and natural places through the very forms of regulation which make the idea of an escape into nature attractive to us in the first place. I argue that parks do not simply 'protect' nature, as we are so often educated to believe, but rather manufacture an experience of wildness and disorder which is not only congruent with widespread practices of environmental toxification, but also plays a central role in constructing particular social relations as 'natural' and 'normal.' The social construction of nature and the policing of 'civilized' social relations are intricately linked.

The Power of Representation

To carry out an examination of the nature of emparkment, it is necessary to engage a theoretical outlook which takes account of how social theory has undergone a paradigm shift in conceptualizing how people are governed in advanced capitalist societies (Hunt 1993:305). Influenced by the writings of Michel Foucault, especially his later writings on 'governmentality' and 'care of the self' (1988, 1991), scholars from a range of interrelated disciplines are rethinking the everyday mechanics of power, forming a movement that can be loosely identified as a 'sociology of governance.'[1] Foucault argued that in the nineteenth century the modern state was 'governmentalized': the exercise of power shifted from the sovereign to what he called an 'art of government,' where individuals could be administered within statistical constructions of population. Closely aligned with the emergence of these 'governmentalities' were the practices of 'police,' what Foucault describes as a governmental technology peculiar to the state. While today the term *police* denotes a specific profession charged with a narrow band of law enforcement, through the seventeenth and early eighteenth centuries the term designated a 'state science' where civic officials administered the experience of citizenship. Described by the police magistrate Patrick Coloquhoun in the early nineteenth century as the 'art of conducting men to the maximum of happiness and the minimum of misery,' police were involved in widespread regulation of habits, trades, commerce, buildings, streets, highways, poverty, peace, and public order (McMullan 1998; see also Gordon 1991: 10). A prominent aspect of emerging 'governmentalities' was the growth of the 'medical police,' with their ever-present themes of public health and sanitation (Carrol 1996). Medical police were also central to the emerging fields of forestry and landscaping, both closely linked to the art of the apothecary. For Foucault (1978), the deployment of medical technologies of governance was to become one of the most important features of modern modes of power, where the human body can be subjected to a wide array of expert gazes.

Marshalled as a category of sociological inquiry, the idea of governance recognizes that political power is exercised 'through a multitude of agencies and techniques, some of which are only loosely associated with the executives and bureaucracies of the formal organs of state' (Miller and Rose 1990:1). This understanding emphasizes the role of 'intellectual technologies' in constructing and regulating individuals from locations that may include, but are not limited to, constitutional governments. To speak of 'government' in this wider sense is to describe an array of mentalities and practices that work to direct social actors and configure individual subjectivity, often in highly peculiar ways that are centred in moralizing programs of self-regulation.[2] This conceptualization of government liberates us from a narrow, instrumentalist view of law which posits a compliant 'subject' that can be commanded, repressed, restricted, and prohibited. Instead, we can consider how social actors, like park destinations, are also 'made up,' this time through a set of discursive trajectories that normalize particular social relations and spaces. Governmental forms of power are primarily positive and constitutive in character: individuals are governed through both the enforcement of particular social roles and identities, such as 'football fan' or 'cancer patient,' as well as more loosely constituted modes or trends of conduct which are congruent with ideas of taste, style, and fashion.

While this approach corrects overly structuralist and materialist conceptions of the state and state power, we should not lose sight of how governmental practices rely on a durable world of stabilized material objects which carry out the representational technologies of knowledge-based expertise. A key aspect of these technologies of power are techniques which construct *visual* representations which in turn enable social actors to moralize individual character and conduct (Law and Whitaker 1988:161). The art of moral regulation, as Rojek points out, has increasingly relied on an expanding repertoire of visualization techniques in an 'age of spectatorship' and in a society dominated by what Mitchell has coined the 'pictorial turn' (Rojek, 1992:356; Mitchell 1994b:16). Terry Eagleton's (1990: 27–8) assertion that morality has become aestheticized as a mode of power brilliantly captures this linkage between visualization and consciousness. 'Power is shifting its location,' writes Eagleton, 'from centralized institutions to the silent, invisible depths of the subject itself ... transforming the relations between law and desire, morality and knowledge ...'

How is the art of moral regulation carried out? The ability of social actors to construct and deploy particular representations relies on processes of translation which carry out what Thévenot (1984) has conceptualized as 'investment in forms.' Thévenot argues for a conception of codes that go beyond the formal texts most often thought of as law to include any set of conventions that order 'regulated' communication. For Thévenot, laws are an especially 'good form' because they stabilize social objects with a minimum of human intervention. Drawing on the work of Ivins (1973), Bruno Latour (1986:7) expands on this notion of investment by exploring the relationship between 'visualization and cognition,' which allows social actors to think 'with eyes and hands.' As Latour reads Ivins: 'no matter from what distance and angle an object is seen, it is always possible to transfer it – to translate it – and to obtain the same object at a different size as seen from another position ... since the picture moves without distortion it is possible to establish, in the linear perspective framework, what he calls a "two way" relationship between object and figure.'

This 'regular avenue through space,' established through this sort of regulatory parallax, is described by Ivins as an 'optical consistency.' Latour (1986, 1987) has brilliantly captured a key expression of this 'two way' relationship through his conceptualization of 'immutable mobiles,' inscriptions that are immutable, combinable, presentable, and mobile, which can be used to 'present absent things.' Immutable mobiles such as statistics, maps, charts, and diagrams allow absent experts and officials to act at a distance from centres of translation and calculation. For Latour, such representations can be deployed within 'socio-technical' networks and constitute a form of domination where 'a few men consider millions as if they were in the palms of their hands' (1986:28). In her discussion of 'textually mediated reality,' Dorothy Smith (1990: 211) discusses how such inscriptions 'speak in the absence of speakers,' detaching meaning from local contexts, producing the 'same' meaning in a 'multiplicity of socially and temporally disjointed settings.' For Smith, the ability of inscriptions to marginalize local forms of knowledge and experience plays a crucial role in oppressive constructions of gender.

A key element in modern representational technologies is the evocation of risk, especially in relation to the deployment of discourses of prevention. Drawing on examples from the history of psychiatry, Robert Castel (1991:282) has noted the shift that has taken place from 'dangerousness to risk,' from the guarding or watching of a specific subject who may cause harm, to a form of power which administers a social field through 'factors, statistical correlations, and heterogeneous elements.' The notion of risk 'becomes autonomous from that of a danger,' writes Castel, and 'A risk does not arise from the presence of particular precise danger embodied in a concrete individual or group. It is the effect of a combination of abstract *factors* which render more or less probable the occurrence of undesirable modes of behaviour' (287). The effect of this shift is that there 'is no longer a subject'; the act of governing relies on acting 'from a distance' and making absent agents present through moralizing discourses (288). Castel argues that this mode of governance has created a vast 'hygienist utopia' where individuals are subjected to a complex of risks which construct individuals within a server asceticism of self-regulation and scrutiny (289). Accompanying this shift from dangerousness to risk is the emergence of the fields of insurance and liability. As a technology of risk (Ewald 1991:198), insurance is not simply a product that can be sold, but rather has become a central form of rationality which underpins neo-liberal fields of welfarist intervention. Pat O'Malley (1991) has discussed in some detail the role of insurance technologies – such as neighbourhood watch programs – in structuring notions of victimization and crime.[3]

Ulrich Beck (1992) has provided a devastating critique of the role of risk representations in constructing how people experience their 'relationship' to nature through the management of environmental toxification. Within a notion of a 'risk society,' Beck attends to the reflexive relationship between 'society and nature' which is mediated by expertise-driven knowledge. Like Latour, Beck argues that scientific knowledge is 'mediated on principle through argument' by scientists who are shaped by particular interests (27, 29). The 'existence and distribution' of risks and hazards are a textually mediated reality, where 'scientific and anti-scientific' knowledge compete by force of argument alone. Risks are 'open to social definition and construction' where extremely hazardous risk positions are often calculated away in the construction of averages, causing an unequal distribution of risk positions (23, 25, 27). 'In their actions and their knowledge,' writes Beck, 'scientists are executors of the generalized social claim to the mastery of nature. When they bend over their material, alone or in regional research laboratories, in a certain sense everyone is looking over their shoulder. When they move their hands, these are the hands of an institution, and in that sense, the hands of all of us' (30). Risk scientists engage in a 'cosmetics' of risk to manage the differences between the risks that are actually posed and the perception of risks (57). A symbolic industry arises, where the sciences become the 'legitimizing patrons of a global industrial pollution and contamination' (59).

In the threatening face of ecological disaster, Beck argues (1992:33), widespread environmental toxification is a hot potato of responsibility that is passed on through expert hands that act physically, without acting morally or politically. 'It is as if one were acting,' comments Beck in an echo of Latour, 'while being personally absent.' The ethics of hegemonic risk production and management involves a 'loss of social thinking' that accompanies the 'industrial pollution of the environment and the destruction of nature' (25). Dependent on the representational technologies of absent experts that act at a distance, individuals lose an essential part of their 'cognitive sovereignty' to the representational techniques of risk managers (54–5).

Beck considers risks to be all radioactivity, toxins, and pollutants that contaminate air, water, and foodstuffs, which in turn create short- and long-term effects on plants, animals, and people. These 'civilization risks' of late modernity were powerfully described by Rachel Carson almost three decades earlier. In her famous work, *Silent Spring* (1962), Carson powerfully evoked the 'grim specter' of a toxified world stricken and silenced by pesticides. Like Beck, Carson communicated the idea of an interdependent ecological community that could be ravaged by the effects of synthetic chemicals. 'There are mysterious and unseen changes,' Carson warns of chemicals, 'by which one alters the power of another for harm' (174).

Condemned by industry as alarmist at the time, Carson's warning about the dangers inherit in agricultural pesticides – most notably, DDT – seems restrained today, especially considering that Carson did not foresee the possibilities for atomic pollution that were most vividly dramatized a decade later at Love Canal. And while Carson evoked a blighted landscape as the inevitable conclusion of widespread toxification, the pollutants of Beck's Risk Society are largely beyond the detection of our own senses, of our 'cognitive sovereignty.' In Beck's vision of late modernity, risks are both more invisible and more dangerous: there is no Silent Spring, no blight across the landscape to warn us of an impending environmental disaster.

For Beck (1992:22, 36), risks are no longer tied to a place or origin; they are global in nature, endangering all life irreversibly, lasting generations. Risks overwhelm the rationality of precaution and insurance. There is no such thing as an atomic accident that can be insured against. The effect will last for generations, the fallout will not respect boundaries of nationhood or class (1992:22, 23). Environmental risks penetrate the everyday to such an extent that a boomerang effect develops: even the rich and powerful cannot hide from the dangers of a toxified society; accumulated risks boomerang back into the very centres of calculation that have set them adrift. However, while risks have a tendency to return to strike back at the very sources of their production – undercutting the profitable infrastructure of risk production – those who lack material and cultural capital still occupy risk positions which are disproportionate. 'Poverty attracts an unfortunate abundance of risks,' Beck reminds us (1992:35). Within this boomerang effect, capital is able to profit from the excess in produced risks: the chemist profits by creating a broad range of synthetic drugs, then profits again by attending to the side effects (such as allergies) that such medication generates.

While risks recede beyond the cognitive ability of individuals, behind a curtain of invisibility which is maintained by the representational technology of scientists, a second movement takes place where pockets of latent side effects begin to emerge into view: holiday lakes quietly acidify, public beaches become awash in oil-soaked birds. Often these side effects are experienced as isolated personal incidents: a childhood beach has been polluted, a favourite tree at the family cottage has died. These environmental 'blank spots' further act to amplify the reflexive character of risk production: local and global political resistance and 'calls for change' force new constructions of risk to emerge in response to a reflexive field of liability and insurance.

Beck (1992: 64–5) is especially outraged at what he calls the 'phony trick' of 'acceptable levels,' which he views as blank checks to 'poison nature and mankind.' Beck argues that acceptable levels of contamination do not prevent pollution, but outline the 'permissible extent of poisoning' (64–5). A world where non-poisoning occurs is 'rejected as utopian' by risk managers, rejected in the construction of a reality where some poisoning is normal and even 'natural.' Our individual bodies become consumer reservoirs where pollutants piggyback into incalculable toxic sequences.

This profitable management of risks is carried out through the deployment of the 'polluter pays principle,' where risks can be presented as local and visible, and an act of polluting can be singled out and blamed. Within what Beck describes as a 'beautiful harmony of science and law,' the 'polluter pays principle' is deployed as 'the channel for recognizing and then dismissing risks' (1992: 63). By finding a strict cause of pollution, located in an individual act, a strict concept of causality is upheld that can be used to disclaim other claims as 'irrational.' For victims of environmental pollution, this upholding of a strict burden of causality represents a purity of scientific analysis, one that minimizes the circle of scientifically valid risks deemed to be officially real. Ironically, the more precisely science is capable of defining a risk, the more likely it is that a wider spectrum of dangers are left outside the circle of official recognition. The movement from dangerousness to risk produces a sphere of abstraction where the corporeal character of social actors is vastly diminished.

Power Scapes

Perhaps the most significant and enduring forms of representation are those which evoke or depict 'the natural.' The construction of nature and the socially constructed character of social relations are intimately linked (Wilson 1992; Merchant 1989; Cosgrove 1984; Zukin 1991). Cultural geographers and historians have focused on the concept of 'landscape' to explore how representations of nature act as modes of power. As W.J. Thomas Mitchell (1994a:2) comments, 'Landscape as a cultural medium thus has a double role with respect to something like ideology: it naturalizes a cultural and social construction, *representing an artificial world as if it were simply given and inevitable,* and it also makes that representation operational by interpellating its beholder in some more or less determinate relation ... landscape [whether urban or rural, artificial or natural]: always greets us as space, as environment, as that *within which "we" (figured as "the figures" in the landscape) find – or lose – ourselves'* (emphasis added).

The ideological content of landscape is vividly captured in Don Mitchell's (1996) study of the early twentieth-century California fruit industry, *The Lie of the Land.* Inspired by John Steinbeck's depiction of depression-era migrant workers in *The Grapes of Wrath,* Mitchell puts forward a 'labour theory of landscape' (9) through an investigation of the struggle between agricultural growers, unions, and the state regulators. In attending to the important link between the actual material production of landscape and the production of landscape representations, Mitchell details how the Californian landscape, depicted by growers and tourism officials as natural and wholesome, could be made possible only through a system of abject poverty, racism, and violence. The postcard image of the rich, bountiful fields was effectively evoked through the visual props of a 'fruit culture' manufactured by well-funded advertising campaigns (19). Mitchell vividly demonstrates Williams's (1973:6) important point that landscape is itself a product of labour that erases any sign of being laboured over. 'Landscape is both a work,' Williams reminds us, 'and an erasure of work.'

As a stable representational form that exists both in the material world and in the 'social imaginary,' landscape works as a powerful instrument of normalization, capturing and disciplining the gaze of the viewer to accept a particular view of social relations. In his analysis of landscape painting, Cosgrove (1984) notes the historical importance of perspective in sustaining an illusion of order so central to how scenes of 'the natural' justify and replicate power relations. Landform features such as trees can be visually manipulated in relation to human-built structures, which construct a notion of social space into which human life can be inserted and ordered (1984:20). According to Cosgrove, perspective then emerged in modernity as a form or mode of truth in itself (21–2), arresting the flow of time and freezing the landscape as a universal reality, while at the same time validating the viewer as the owner or holder of that image. As Williams (1973:87) commented in relation to the shift to anti-pastoral forms of poetry, landscape can be changed by an alteration of a particular way of seeing. The ability of a stabilized perspective to represent reality is central to Latour's emphasis on 'optical consistency,' where social relations and spaces can be ordered and homogenized. As Cosgrove (1984:26) comments, perspective 'offers a view of the world directed at the experience of one individual at a given moment in time when the arrangement of the constituent forms is pleasing, uplifting or in some other way linked to the observers psychological state; it then represents this view as universally valid by claiming for it the status of reality.'

John Urry (1990) argues that the visual perspective constructed by tourist mentalities – what he refers to as a 'tourist gaze' – is a more contemporary example of the power of perspective, which homogenizes local economies and commodifies landscape. According to Turner and Ash (1975), the use of photography has displaced landscape painting as the central way in which visual reality is constructed and represented to serve the 'golden horde' of global tourism, a trend Aldo Leopold (1966: 263–4) recognized when he suggested, in his *A Sand County Almanac*, that photography was a type of 'trophy' hunting, although one that was much less destructive than the damage brought by hunters and fishermen.

As a specific mode of landscape, emparkment can be understood as an assembly of practices where space is enclosed under legislative authority in such a way that it represents an ideal of the natural that has the effect of representing 'an artificial world as if it were simply given.' The practice of emparking can be considered a primary representational technology where the heterogeneous qualities of nature are translated into a sanitized, ordered, homogeneous landscape that people are figured within. The park visitors 'sight' is emparked as well, ensuring that an altered state of seeing is normalized and rendered universal in the 'scene.'

In the late nineteenth century, the first parks established in North America, while congruent with preservationist sentiments of the time, were formed out of a complex of concerns regarding timber and water preservation, public recreation, and notions of social hygiene. The emergence of scientific forestry techniques in the 1870s provided industry with a powerful set of management tools to argue for timber and water reserves, and assemblies such as the American Forestry Congress provided a forum for commercial timber and agricultural interests.[4] Perhaps most importantly, the idea of the park as a place of refreshment and rejuvenation had lodged in the public imagination at a time of widespread anxiety about the moral character of urban life. Established in 1872, Yellowstone was created as a 'pleasure ground for the benefit and enjoyment of the people' (Lowry 1994). In Canada,

Rocky Mountain Park at Banff closely followed the mission of Yellowstone when it was founded in 1887 (it was first a reserve in 1885) as a 'public park and pleasure ground for the benefit, advantage, and enjoyment of people' (Lowry 1994:95; Marty 1984:62). In 1893, in legislation which closely followed that of Banff, Algonquin National park was established as a 'public park and forest reservation, fish and game preserve, health resort and pleasure ground for the benefit, advantage and enjoyment of people of the Province' (Killan 1993:15). These 'pleasure ground' parks did not simply arise from an emerging twentieth-century tourist culture; rather, they were the product of a complex of emparkment practices which were deeply embedded in the institutions of Western power.

In seventeenth- and eighteenth-century England, parliamentary acts of enclosure created private emparkments and dispossessed thousands of rural inhabitants. The abolishment of common spaces such as pastures and roads, and the use of game laws to restrict hunting to landholding gentry, destroyed the means of subsistence for a poor rural population. Customary rights affecting grazing, the collection of firewood (especially lops and tops of trees and deadwood), and access to clay, stones, and heath were severely restricted or in some cases abolished altogether. The most notorious of the laws which accompanied private enclosures was the Black Act, passed in 1723, which created fifty new capital offences for those who blackened their faces to raid on private emparked areas, royal chases, and forests. E.P. Thompson (1990) vividly describes the malicious extent to which customary usages were withdrawn and rural inhabitants persecuted, and how the 'blacks,' often highly organized and mounted, ran a running battle of 'agrarian warfare' with forest officers.

These enclosure practices had the effect of configuring landscape and 'figuring' targets of regulation in such a way that relations of power and domination were 'naturalized' as a normal, given order. 'It is ironic,' comments Short (1991:67), 'that the typical English countryside, the supercharged image of English environmental ideology, which can still conjure up notions of community, unchanging values and national sentiments, is in reality the imprint of a profit based exercise which destroyed the English peasantry and replaced a moral economy of traditional rights and obligations with the cash nexus of commercial capitalism.'

It is a great irony that one of the major architects of the urban park movement in the United States was inspired by the emparked character of the English countryside. Accompanied by his brother and a close friend, Frederick Law Olmsted travelled throughout England for thirteen weeks in the summer of 1850, recording details about an array of interests ranging from soil drainage and beet cultivation to the manners and language of the labouring poor. Most of all, Olmsted was deeply moved by what he saw of England's countryside and parks, and felt that they provided an example for America. 'Probably there is no object of art that Americans of cultivated taste more generally long to see in Europe, than an English park,' Olmsted wrote after his walk through Eaton Park. 'What artist, so noble, has often been my thought, as he who, with far-reaching conception of beauty and designing power, sketches the outline, writes the colours, and directs the shadows of a picture so great that Nature shall be employed upon it for generations ...' (Olmsted 1852). Olmsted seems to have had little understanding of the oppressive property relations which inscribed the emparkments that he praised so heavily for their 'civic' value. Certainly, he was inordinately drawn to the quaint and picturesque, even to the point that he remained relatively unimpressed with the great cathedrals and halls to which his guidebook directed him (137). Guided by this romanticized view, Olmsted was within the decade the most influential landscape architect in North America. At the centre of his work was an explicit concern with the 'civic' values of park space, which he believed English emparkments to embody. Olmsted's most celebrated project was the designing of Central Park in New York City, but he also designed countless other parks across North America as part of the 'rational recreationist' and playground movement.[5] Urban parks went hand in hand with a variety of projects of moral improvement and civic sanitation where open space, fresh air, and available sunshine were considered vital for the moral conditioning of the soul.

Closely linked to the enclosure practices of the powerful British aristocracy which re-inscribed the English countryside was the establishment of nature preserves in colonial Africa. Several historians (Grove 1990, Neumann 1996, MacKenzie 1986, 1988) have documented how African wildlife was to be preserved as an 'imperial inheritance.' 'The control over nature,' writes Neumann (1998:95), 'must be recognized as an integral part of the geography and history of empire.' Preserve and park making dislocated tens of thousands of peasants, devastated local economies, and, through the introduction of game laws, allowed a select group of Europeans entitlement to hunt while constructing local efforts of food harvesting as acts of 'poaching' (MacKenzie 1988:68). A specific construction of nature was vital to the colonizing power of imperial Britain, first in the use of game reserves and then through more specific acts of park making.

Patrician conservationists drew on an ideal or rural idyll of the emparked nature of enclosed countryside, while at the same time appealing to the success of national parks founded in America and the colonies. Neumann argues that colonial parks played an important hegemonic role, not only in asserting imperial administration on local native culture but also in dramatizing imperial values at a time when the power base of the aristocracy was crumbling after the First World War (Neumann 1998). This 'world vision' of colonial nature control was most vividly expressed through a number of preservation societies, most notably the Society for the Preservation of the Fauna of the Empire (SPFE). Founded in 1903, the society was composed of aristocrats who were at the centre of colonial administration at the turn of the century (81). Key elements of British colonial ideology – racial superiority and a civilizing mission – were at the core of the preserves they emparked (92), and the society demonstrated a racism which viewed native reserves as a model for the preservation of 'wild and savage animals.' As its president, the Earl of Onslow suggested in a meeting of the society in 1928: 'In all colonies native reserves have been established and the analogy of the native reserve might possibly be followed in regard to the wild animals, and reserves for the wild animals placed on the same basis as those for the indigenous population' (SPFE 1928:26).

Like the rest of the colonial landscape, preserves were to benefit from white attendance and supervision. Despite their por-
trayal of natives as savage simpletons, white managers were often
forced to employ native assistants to run the parks, a fact that was
a constant point of irritation, as cited in the preservationist literature. Natives were not only considered untrustworthy, but it was
believed they also could not be counted on to carry out the
'chronology' of imperial justice. As one colonial preserve manager explained: 'People often say, "Why do you use native Scouts
to watch and catch white men?" Nobody regrets the necessity to
use native scouts more than I do. They have no idea of chrono-
logical sequence, and in consequence frequently contradict each
other in matters of detail. They tell their stories in court in a
manner which suggests a "frame up," but the essence of the story
is usually true. If we had adequate staff, we could have a white man
near the spot, and he could investigate the case then and there,
obtain proper evidence, and take what action was necessary' (SPFE
1924:49). At the core of this racist notion of nature preservation
was the idea of The Hunt as an enlightened activity, one that was
considered a fair and legitimate sport. Traditional methods of
game harvest, which involved elaborate social and technical knowledge, were demonized by the society and depicted in their literature as savage and cruel (SPFE 1930a:51).

While patrician notions of conservation and trophy hunting
were anchored in the emparked character of the English countryside, the idea of establishing parks as distinct from preserves grew
out of the admiration colonial managers had for the parks in
North America. The society paid a great deal of attention to the
progress of newly formed parks such as Yellowstone and Banff,
and established a global network of contacts where members
visited and shared information with one another (81). In 1928 the
president of the society, the Earl of Onslow, noted that the parks
in Canada and New Zealand, which had 'the finest scenery in the
Dominion,' were financially sound, as 'they are becoming the
holiday resorts for people of the towns' (SPFE 1928:26).[6] In 1926
the first park in anglophone Africa, Kruger National Park, was

established in South Africa. In arguing the importance of the national parks being based on the example of those in North America, Colonel Stevenson-Hamilton described national parks 'in which the reserves or sanctuaries become stabilized by legislation in such a manner that they cannot be abolished at the mere passing whim of any government temporarily in power' (SPFE 1930b:14). Parks were beginning to be seen as distinct from preserves, thus reflecting a paradigm shift away from the concerns of the hunting elite and towards what was becoming a tourist elite. This shift fundamentally changed the anthropomorphic aesthetics of park animal attractiveness: lions, formerly considered vermin to be exterminated, now became valued signifiers for a preserved African wild. Kruger Park administrators soon developed a system of roadways which tourists could travel for a price, a development which also required a system for issuing permits. As Stevenson-Hamilton noted in a society journal article, 'The permits contain a printed list of prohibitions, such as shooting with or interfering with animals, destroying trees, burning grass, and so on, and a leaflet is issued with each permit containing a list of "Don'ts" for the benefit of persons who have only a rudimentary acquaintance with wilder Africa' (SPFE 1930b:19).

The use of permits represented a refinement of the system of licensing used in preserves, which created a 'permitted' park user. These permitted parks played a major role in establishing tourism as a legitimate goal of post-colonial economies, and opened the way for the invasion of the 'golden hordes' of western tourists (Turner and Ash 1975).

The emergence of North American 'pleasure parks' in the late nineteenth century emerged from a kind of spatial economy of emparkment forms where exploitative social relations were normalized as part of a natural order through the specific emparkment practices of enclosures, preserves, reserves, and parks. The English countryside, inscribed with the power relations of the aristocracy, become a pastoral ideal for colonial parks in Africa and for urban parks in America, while North American pleasure parks provided a new model with which to administer the imperial legacy of 'colonial' nature, which then could be experienced through white European eyes. Emparkment techniques rested at the very heart of the exercise of Western power.

Regulating Eden

At the beginning of the twenty-first century, how do North American parks represent an official version of nature at a time of widespread environmental destruction? And how can we understand the practices of emparkment as a form of power central to everyday experience, where the presentation of 'the natural' is intricately linked to notions of order and freedom? This book explores these questions by examining the ways in which park laws and policy structure the experience of 'the natural' in North American parks. Though I have placed an analysis of formal law and government policy at the centre of my analysis, I should not be mistaken for one of those who posit 'the state' as some all-powerful entity, some 'cold monster' that directs social life, a caricature that many followers of Foucault employ to dismiss the presence of the state from theories of power altogether. I reject 'the state' as a reified object of sociological inquiry, just as I reject a positivist conception of the law as a textual monolith which is autonomous from social life. I do, however, recognize the state as a site where often unintended and contradictory projects of moral order are generated, often in very peculiar and unintended ways. This approach has allowed me to focus on what Philip Abrams has conceptualized as 'politically organized subjection' which carries out the 'actualities of social subordination.' As Abrams (1988:82) says, 'The state comes into being as a structuration within political practice; it starts life as an implicit construct; it is then reified – as the *res publica*, the public reification, no less – and acquires an overt symbolic identity progressively divorced from practice as an illusory account of practise ... The task of the sociologist is to demystify; and in this context that means attending to the senses in which the state does not exist rather than to those in which it does.'

To extend Abrams's argument, we should attend to ways that the law does not exist, in the sense that we should be critical about the ways in which the deployment of the idea of 'the law' obscures and masks subtle and peculiar ways in which normalizing practices take place. A complement of this approach is a resistance to take part in the sterile debate around the questions of law as being 'important' or 'unimportant,' an unproductive distinction which obscures the ways in which legal discourses are imbricated in the very grain of social life. By adopting a necessarily complex notion of law which views everyday governance as complex and contradictory, we can accept that the law can simultaneously appear to be both trivial and important, both mundane and sacred. By utilizing a notion of government which embraces state practices as one of many competing complexes of governance, we can best examine the ways in which (to paraphrase Abrams), 'state' parks *state* an official version of nature through discourses of moral order.

This book carries out a detailed examination of park legislation and policy from across North America. While I focus primarily on a wide selection of park legislation, I also review other park-governance documents such as training materials, internal policy and public relations materials, field orders, and personal correspondence from selected jurisdictions. I take a discursive stand in the analysis of this documentation, attending to the metaphors and tropes, contradictions and paradoxes, tensions and homologies that occur within these intersecting materials. I am specifically interested in how these texts intersect in discourses, in 'organized sets of signifying practices' (Valverde 1991:10) that have the effect of representing nature. Such an approach is appropriate, considering the textually mediated, multifaceted character of 'the law,' which I view as being constantly mediated and authored within the power relations of everyday life. As Paulus (1974:10), has noted, laws do not 'arise full-grown children of the dragon's teeth,' they often unravel in the relations and spaces of social life in ways that their creators could never foresee, much less desire. I am interested in the overarching architecture of how nature is ordered in parks, and, conversely, how the notion of order is in itself produced in places that are attractive to us in our everyday lives because they appear permissive, peaceful, and thus natural.

Some explanation is needed about the type and range of the parks I have examined. This book deals with parks that are an expression of national, state, or provincial interest, parks we typically think of as 'recreational parks,' places we visit on weekend camping trips and family holidays. While much park policy goes to great lengths to make distinctions between 'recreational parks' and those that are more environmentally worthy, I consider state or provincial parks as recreational if they permit members of the public to enter and engage in some form of leisure activity. Indeed, as I hope will become clear, I view forms of designation which differentiate between 'recreational' and 'nature' parks as largely artificial in character within the current ethos of 'park management.'

By lumping such a range of parks together in my analysis, am I not eradicating important local, geographic, political, and economic differences? Can I really compare parks that feature golf courses and bungee jumping with those that offer thousands of acres of roadless forested area? The answer lies in the observation that the regulations that govern these diverse sites are nevertheless remarkably similar in character. It seems to me that the significant question becomes: How do emparkment practices homogenize and commodify local landscapes in a way that manufactures an emparkment aesthetic which signifies a 'natural' and wild experience?

This book is concerned with the overall architecture of nature construction in North American park destinations. I focus on what appears at first to be the mundane, obvious forms of regulation such as the 'no littering' sign, features that we might, at first glance, dismiss as trivial or unimportant. In chapter 2 I investigate the legislative missions of parks and the often flawed character of the park rangers who carry out such missions. I then examine, in Chapter 3, how these missions are expressed through the regulation of park space, and discuss the main techniques used to mediate wild landscapes. Chapter 4 explores in some detail how the conduct of park visitors is ordered, with a view to manufacturing wilderness experiences, especially in relation to fire and alcohol. In the concluding chapter I argue that emparked nature produces discourses of risk that legitimize widespread environmental destruction. I also explore how the regulated wilderness of park destinations has consequences for the ordering of the everyday, consequences that go way beyond the boundaries of the places we believe to be wild.

CHAPTER TWO

The Ranger Mission

I recognize the badge of the Oklahoma State Park as a symbol of public faith, and I accept it as a public trust to be held so long as I am true to the ethics of the public service. I will constantly strive to achieve these objectives and ideals, dedicating myself before God to my chosen profession ... outdoor ... recreation ... and ... visitor ... protection.

Oklahoma State Ranger Code of Ethics

As the sworn agent of emparkment missions, the park ranger patrols the boundaries of park destinations, policing a notion of order that is peculiar to North American parks. Park rangers do much more than simply 'preserve and protect' park resources and users; they enforce a regime of permission that is central to the presentation of the park as a 'natural' landscape. This chapter explores the character of the park ranger and the mission which he is charged with carrying out.

Considering the wide variety of emparkment projects in North America, it is somewhat surprising that there appears to be a reasonably unambiguous category of park employee who is charged with enforcing park regulations. Most generally, rangers are distinct from other park employees because they are invested with police-like powers and have a job description which includes a law-enforcement component. Specifically, rangers occupy an occupational category within the larger field of fisheries, game, and environmental law enforcement.

The figure of the park ranger or forest ranger has come to occupy a significant position in North American culture, as lonely figures that mediate between the 'human' and the 'natural.' The lookout or fire-tower ranger is the archetype of the ranger persona, a figure who watches over thousands of acres of forest, mapping lightening strikes and counting the distance between thunderclaps from an isolated tower. Despite the fact that fire-tower and lookout rangers are distinct from rangers that actively patrol parks,[1] the two types are blurred together in the popular imagination. The lookout ranger, also often associated with a romantic view of nature as a conquered wilderness, is perhaps most famously dramatized in Jack Kerouac's novel *Desolation Angels* (1965). Working as a fire lookout at Desolation Peak in northwest Washington, the writer most closely associated with the beat generation was deeply traumatized by the harrowing loneliness and isolation of his mountain lookout, an experience from which he was never able to fully recover. A week before the job ended, Kerouac wrote: 'I learned that I hate myself because by myself I am only myself ... I go mad one afternoon thinking like this, only one week to go and I don't know what to do with myself ... I want to return at once, sitting at a stool with a hamburger, lighting a butt with coffee, let there be rain on redbrick walls and I got a place to go and poems to write about hearts not just rocks – Desolation Adventure finds me finding at the bottom of myself abysmal nothingness worst than that no illusion even – my mind's in rags' (Kerouac 1971:78). The inner torment faced by Kerouac powerfully dramatizes the link between madness and wilderness that is so deeply entrenched in Western conceptions of nature.

Norman Maclean strikes a somewhat lighter note in his book *A River Runs Through It*, where he recounts his summer job as a lookout at a time when 'they still picked rangers for the forest service by picking the toughest guy in town' (1976:126). In his struggle to prove himself and be accepted by his male peers, Maclean emerges from his summer experience not only with more confidence in himself, but also with an awareness of the frail, transient character of human relationships. Maclean's telling of his lookout experience touches on a major theme in North

American culture: the sending of young men into nature for the summer (the summer camp, Boy Scouts, Junior Ranger programs) as a rite of passage into adulthood.

More popular depictions of rangers throughout the 1960s and 1970s in television shows such as the *Young Forest Rangers* portray rangers as kind, nature-smart helpers. These characterizations were central to the Walt Disney family room depictions of nature popularized by an array of Wild Kingdom-style nature programs (Wilson 1992). The image of the kindly ranger was also often linked with highly anthropomorphic presentations of apparently 'wild' animals imbued with human qualities. The apex of these presentations was probably the popular Hanna-Barbera cartoon depicting the fictional 'Jellystone National Park.' Certainly, Ranger Dave's bumbling efforts to carry out spot checks on the picnic baskets of Yogi Bear and Boo-Boo became the prominent impression of the activities of the park ranger to a generation of North American parks users.

Considering the distinctly American character of the cultural stereotype of the ranger, is there anything different about the agents of Canadian emparkment projects? Gaile McGregor, in her effort to delineate 'the morphology of the Canadian langscape' (1985:10), probes the difference between Canadian and American representations of nature. Attending to how artistic expression acts to mythicize the environment in a way which generates a readable cultural field, what McGregor calls a 'langscape,' she argues that Canadian culture resonates with a deep fear of wilderness, where a 'view from the fort' dominates the Canadian view of nature. McGregor names this tendency the Wacousta syndrome, after the title of John Richardson's late-nineteenth-century wilderness romance novel. This negative view of nature expressed in Canadian culture is fundamentally different from the American representations of nature as a malevolent garden to be explored and colonized. McGregor notes that, unlike the Edenic imagery of American landscapes, Canadian representations rarely depict nature as a garden.[2]

Can we detect a Wacousta syndrome in the character of Canadian 'rangers' and the emparkment gaze which they police? In a very tentative way, we can. Most obviously, the preferred Canadian title of warden is distinct from the almost universal title of ranger, used by American jurisdictions. The title 'warden' evokes the image of a more pastoral agent who watches over a specific 'ward' located in an institution such as a hospital or prison. The term is historically linked with the activity of a 'keeper,' someone who watches over a particular jurisdiction. The French title of Ontario's park wardens, 'Gardiens du Parks,' captures this connotation of stewardship more closely.

In contrast, the American term *rangers* suggests a more paramilitary, outward-looking individual who actively wanders across a venturesome landscape. This wandering quality of American rangers is vividly expressed in the much greater role the American National Park Service (NPS) has taken in the formation of a collective national memory, a quality enshrined in the Antiquities Act of 1906, which enables the president to establish national monuments (Miles 1995:7). The result has been sites such as the Vietnam memorial in Washington, D.C., and there is nothing as monumental or ambitious in the Parks Canada system that compares. With the exception of a number of military forts and canal systems, the Canadian emparkment gaze is much more modest and less adventurous then the American, which emparks across a much larger, more emotionally charged 'langscape.'

This distinction can be traced to the genesis of park policing in each country. In the United States, the American military occupied and policed Yosemite, Sequoia, and General Grant Parks from the time of their establishment, and were called into Yellowstone in 1886 to protect the park from rampant poaching and forest fires (Marty 1984; Ise 1961:208). The army was withdrawn from parks by 1914, triggering the establishment of the National Park Service in 1916, five years later than the Canadian Park Service was established. After a congressional dispute over the funding of the new park service, a ranger force was established in 1918 comprising twenty-five field staff, many of whom left the army to join up with the new civilian service (Ise 1961:208, Rettie 1995:153). As the 'forerunner of the park service,' the army left behind a formidable infrastructure of built projects, and the new park staff adopted army-style uniforms and continued on with military park management practices (Sellars 1997; Everhart 1983). Runte (1987) convincingly argues that early American parks such as Yosemite and Yellowstone were largely a cultural rather than an environmental phenomenon, one that was closely linked to questions of national identity. The discovery of the Yosemite Valley and Sierra redwoods in 1851–52 'provided the first believable evidence since Niagara Falls that the United States had a valid claim to cultural recognition through natural wonders' (19). The mentality of monumentalism, which was given great authority by the military presence of the cavalry, was given even more vivid expression in the establishment in 1872 of Yellowstone, a place which offered what Runte describes as a 'semblance of antiquity through landscape' (41).

In contrast, the first 'national' park in Canada, at Banff, was initially patrolled by the North Western Mounted Police, supplemented by some part-time wardens during the summer. In 1909 the 'Fire and Game Guardian Service' – later known as the Park Warden Service – was established under the National Park General Regulations, which enabled the appointment of 'game guardians' with police-like powers to protect the park against poaching and fire. The first squad of guardians consisted of three men outfitted with tin badges and Stetson hats, who were charged with policing forty-two square miles of park (Marty 1984: 86). Unlike their American colleagues, however, the Park Warden Service never displaced the initial mounted police force.

The result is that Canadian wardens, at both provincial and federal levels, police a much narrower band of conduct more closely associated with a park management ethos, on sites which are much less culturally monumental then American sites. Unlike their American colleagues, Canadian wardens rarely conduct criminal investigations in parks, and are usually distinct from conservation officers who carry out fish and game law enforcement. There seems to be little evidence, however, that Canadian wardenship has more consistently exercised preservationist values, as some commentators have suggested. From the beginning, the managers of parks such as Banff and Algonquin were as keen to invite

resource exploitation into the parks as were their American colleagues.

Today, park rangers and wardens are no longer the jacks of all
trades that Norman Maclean describes, but are college and university educated, and are often given intensive law enforcement
training (Rettie 1995:154). While the 'lookout' ranger, like the
lighthouse keeper on ocean coasts, has been displaced by an
array of remote sensing technology, there has been a marked
shift in the last decade from forestry educated park rangers who
worked within a 'resource management' tradition, to a new
breed of park officer who view themselves as simply another
branch of the law enforcement establishment. Nevertheless, the
idea of a figure that stands over and watches a wilderness remains a powerful part of the public expectation of how parks are
policed and ordered.

Regulating Exploitation

Park ranger appointments[3] originate in provincial and state legislation, which establishes the statutory authority of park jurisdictions and designates officers to act for the purpose of park
legislation. It is important to note that most park rangers are
appointed within park legislation itself, as part of an overarching
program of resource management. It is notable, for example, that
I have rarely come across an instance where the words *police* or
park police are used as titles for park enforcement staff.[4]

What is known as the mission statement plays a major role in
guiding policy and rationalizing administrative decisions. Mission
statements are considered 'a widely shared and approved understanding of the central tasks of the agency' (Lowry 1994:31). In
interviewing national park service employees in both Canada and
the United States, Lowry found that the mission statement was
almost a mantra for park employees, and was appealed, cited, and
recounted in a variety of situations to justify and rationalize agency
activity. By focusing on the park ranger, I do not mean to suggest
that rangers are solely responsible for the operation of these
mandates; the 'mission' of park legislation guides a broad range

of field and administrative agents. However, rangers are intimately connected to these statements of purpose because they rely on them to codify and rationalize their power and authority.

The 'purpose,' 'objective,' 'mission,' or 'mandate' that constitutes park jurisdictions and appoints park rangers is expressed either directly, in enabling legislation, or is stated in policy that is the product of a process authorized by public law. Often dedicated 'to the people,'[5] mission statements are extraordinary for their use of vague and sweeping language. Parks exist for human 'happiness,' for the 'shelter, comfort and education of people' (Pennsylvania A:s.1906A.(3)), 'for greater development of their cultural and physical potential' (Louisiana A:s.101A), 'to stimulate the health and welfare of man' (Montana B:s.75-1-01) – goals which are often said to be secured for the sake of 'future generations' (Ontario A:s.2). The utopian tone of park missions is remarkable: parks are visualized as places of self-improvement, rejuvenation, and regeneration for both the human and natural world. The recent emphasis on programs of 'physical fitness' in outdoor settings has strengthened this historical link between healthful rejuvenation and park settings.

More specifically, mission statements express two general goals that are unproblematically posed as being complementary and interdependent: the preservation and protection of environmental resources, and the provision of these resources for public consumption through the management of recreational activities. Michigan provides a typical example, that the state

create, maintain, operate, and make available for public use and enjoyment a system of state parks to preserve and protect Michigan's significant natural resources and areas of natural beauty or historic significance, to provide open space for public recreation and to provide an opportunity to understand Michigan's natural resources. (Michigan D)[6]

And in the Yukon:

The Executive Council may establish a system of parks to protect unique, natural and historic features and provide for comprehensive outdoor recreational opportunities. (Yukon A:s.26)

A minority of mission statements more specifically target the regulation of visitor conduct within this preservation/recreation dynamic. For example:

The purpose ... is to govern the conduct of visitors to state lands and to provide for the protection of the natural resources.' (Wisconsin A:s.45.01)

The province of British Columbia is even more explicit about the public use of park areas:

[T]he Parks Branch has jurisdiction over, and shall manage and administer, all matters concerning ... the *preservation*, development, use and maintenance of parks and recreation areas and natural resources on and in them; the regulation and control of public and private individuals in the *use or exploitation of parks and recreation areas and the natural resources in and on them*, and of human activities, behaviour and conduct in or on parks and recreation areas. (British Columbia F:s.3(1); emphasis added)

This regulated exploitation of the park landscape and resources requires that 'nature' be constructed and depicted in a way that presents preservation and recreation as mutually compatible goals which will result in a 'natural' harmony, as illustrated in this mandate:

The purpose ... is to declare a state policy which will encourage productive and enjoyable harmony between man and his environment, to promote efforts which will *prevent or eliminate damage to the environment* and biosphere and stimulate the health and welfare of man. (Montana A:s.75-1-01; emphasis added)

And in Colorado:

It is the policy of the state of Colorado that the wildlife and their
environment are to be protected, preserved, *enhanced*, and managed for the use, benefit, and enjoyment of the people of this state
and its visitors. (Colorado C:33-1-101(1))

As constituted in park legislation, park jurisdictions are not
only supposed to facilitate an 'enjoyable harmony' between nature and 'man,' but can actually 'enhance' nature and 'eliminate
damage to the environment.'[7] This sentiment, that parks can
somehow *repair* a damaged environment, has a parallel in the
questionable idea that urban trees are the 'lungs of the city' – that
trees can fight air pollution – a notion that Jane Jacobs has called
'science fiction nonsense' (Jacobs 1961:91). The establishment of
a park, in the legislators' imagination, seems to imply a gesture of
undoing past environmental exploitation and making up for past
environmental 'sins,' that parks are constructed as sites of pen-
ance where people can atone for a wasteful and unnatural lifestyle
which is carried out in the perceived corruption of non-park
space.

In ordering the practices of 'regulated exploitation,' park rangers promote an image of nature that is amenable to the recreation, entertainment, and enjoyment of humans. In park law,
environmental preservation and recreation are woven into one
another; park space is constructed as always having been a 'wild'
area, a place where human activities, including regulated recreation, are inserted as an inherent quality of nature itself. This
construction of nature as an object of consumer culture is vividly
portrayed in an illustration used to promote Minnesota State Park
Rules (see Figure 1), where 'nature' is depicted in the archetypal
figure of a tree that is 'made up' by a collage of recreational
activities. Within this image of preserved nature, the use of nature
for recreational activities is preserved as well. A park 'going public' is predominantly illustrated with the image of a 'normal'
heterosexual family with children, an image that constantly appears in the literature as part of an emphasis on the value of
'family camping.' The regulated public is depicted as being as

'natural' as the crown and branches of the tree under which a family recreates. The image of this 'rule tree' serves as a powerful emblem of the 'regulated exploitation' endorsed by park missions. Consumerism has found a perfect site in ruled park space, where both the past and future are preserved in an emblem which celebrates a present of often environmentally degrading recreations.

The timeless, preserved quality of this regulated wilderness requires that the constructed, 'man-made' and 'mandated' nature of park space be obscured and masked, that parks be seen as synonymous with nature. This discursive intent is vividly expressed in a Pennsylvania Administrative Code of 1929 which remains in force:

> the ... shelter, comfort and education of people shall be so designed and constructed as to retain, so far as may be, the naturalistic appearance of State park areas, surroundings and approaches, and *conceal the hand of man as ordinarily visible* in urban, industrial and commercial activities. (Pennsylvania A:s.A(3); emphasis added)

As the appointed agents of park missions, rangers are burdened with an inherently contradictory role: to promote park space as 'natural' and 'wild,' and to 'conceal the hand of man' that designs and constructs park space, while at the same time 'revealing' the park as a place amenable to 'man's' enjoyment and recreation. Closely linked to the discourses of 'public safety and security' is the emphasis on visitor education: park rangers are expected to carry out education in a context of 'prevention,' where visitors are informed of inappropriate behaviour that might harm themselves and the 'natural' features of the park. As educators, rangers are expected to evoke the powerful trope of 'heritage,' to communicate 'values' that exemplify a 'harmonious' relationship between humans and nature, often expressed in the idea of 'stewardship' and 'resource management.' For example:

> [The Washington State Parks and Recreation Commission] is re-

Figure 1 From a brochure to promote Minnesota State Park Rules
(Courtesy of the Minnesota Department of Natural Resources)

sponsible for the long term care and protection of the statewide
system of parks belonging to the people of the state of Washington.
The agency's dual mission is to provide for recreation ... and enjoyment of this large and diverse parks system, while providing *good
stewardship necessary to ensure values which the system represents are held
intact for future generations.* (Washington A; emphasis added)

As educators, rangers are often cast as representing and 'holding
intact' a value system which both preserves and provides access to
nature. This pervading notion of 'good stewardship' relies on the
evocation of a nostalgia of a lost past, of an idea of community
where common values are exercised for the benefit of future
generations.

'Good Enforcement Is Good Hosting'

The emparkment mission or mandate of park jurisdictions, to
both preserve nature and provide recreational opportunities, is
operationalized in the construction of two contradictory park
ranger roles: the ranger is a professional 'law enforcer' who pro-
tects nature through the policing of visitor conduct; he/she is also
expected to be a thoughtful 'host' who facilitates recreational
opportunities. This tension between law enforcement and hospi-
tality is aggravated by the manner in which ranger programs
adopt police-like mentalities in carrying out the job, making rangers less likely to participate in activities that are not congruent
with the image of a 'real' law enforcer. Thus, in prescribing ranger
conduct, park administrators seem to struggle with the question:
how do we provide park rangers with police 'power,' police training, police-like ranks, police weapons, police assistance – all of
which they need to carry out our ambiguous, even utopian mission – yet make sure that they don't behave like police officers and
offend park visitors, whose visits we rely on to fulfil our purpose?

A widespread tactic in reducing the conflict posed by these
simultaneous roles is to emphasize a 'low-key' *attitude* that rangers
should take in dealing with the public. 'Law enforcement procedure,' suggests a Georgia manual, 'requires a low-key approach

wherever possible, and emphasizes management actions that will discourage inappropriate or illegal behaviour. Park officers are not "park police," but resource managers' (Georgia C:5). And in West Virginia: 'The goal ... is to keep law enforcement very low key, and issue citations only when absolutely necessary. Law enforcement activities are considered to be one tool that area management staff has to ensure maximum use and efficiency for park guests' (West Virginia A).[8]

In this 'low-key' mode, rangers are urged to practice 'public relations' (Niagara Parks Commission B; Maryland C), 'public service' (Washington A), 'visitor service,' 'customer relations' (Wisconsin B) and 'patron involvement' (Kansas A) in dealing with the public. Rangers are trained in 'the art of being nice' and 'service effectiveness' (Wisconsin B), are encouraged to be 'polite but firm,' 'user friendly,' 'friendly, courteous, helpful and informed,' and to greet 'everyone with a smile' (Alberta A:2). The attempt to reconcile a law enforcer role with that of a smiling, friendly host is vividly demonstrated in a Province of Alberta training document, ironically titled 'The Park Law Enforcer': 'While the need for regulations has always been apparent, sometimes the need to enforce them is not. Why is this the case? Why is enforcement sometimes looked upon as a bad word? One reason is that some feel the enforcement role of the Park Ranger is just not compatible with a proper "Good Host" image. This is definitely not the case. *Good Enforcement Is Good Hosting.* To be a "Good Host," Park Rangers not only welcome people to parks but they also provide for their safety and security' (Alberta A; emphasis original).

However, this emphasis backfires when the policy writer worries that rangers may go too far in being non-confrontational 'hosts' and neglect their duties as law enforcers. In a rather paranoid passage a few paragraphs later the rangers are warned:[9] 'As "Good Hosts," Park Rangers welcome visitors to the parks, just as you and I welcome visitors to our homes. They do not, however, allow their visitors to get drunk and disorderly, vandalize and destroy property, steal, physically or sexually assault others, endanger the safety of others, cause a disturbance by yelling and screaming or otherwise ruin the enjoyable visit of other visitors ... do you?' (Alberta B; ellipsis original).

Yet, another park manager worries about the possibility of zealous rangers who *really do* consider the park 'their homes,' when in fact the park belongs 'to the people.' Under the instructive heading, 'Dont's: The Helpful Variety,' an Oklahoma manual states: '*Don't Lecture*. It is calamitous from a public relations standpoint for an officer to lecture an offender. State parks are not the property of the officer – [the parks] belong to all the people. You are the protector – not the judge nor the high executioner. Do not humiliate an offender, nor cause him/her to lose face' (Oklahoma A:113).[10]

These passages nicely reflect the bizarre consequences of encouraging officers to be tough law enforcers who are also expected to serve as friendly hosts to vacationing tourists. Certainly, the extent to which rangers should carry out law enforcement work has become one of the most contentious issues in park management circles. As Everhart (1983:54) comments concerning American parks, 'The fact that the Yosemite pistol team regularly outshoots all other police organizations in California is a matter of some pride, but it may be too much to ask that rangers who wear guns and are professionally competent in conducting criminal investigations be equally proficient on bird identifications and the niceties of forest ecology.'[11]

The deep contradiction of the preservation/recreation mission translates operationally into two competing discourses that constantly collide and intersect in the practices of park governance: a mission of recreation where rangers are hosts who treat visitors as customers, and a mission of preservation where rangers are law enforcers who treat visitors as violators. Thus, it is not unusual in training manuals to find a section entitled 'enforcement philosophy' that encourages a 'good host' mentality, and one further on that instructs officers on activities such as car chases, arrest techniques, and the use of handcuffs and offensive weapons. Park agents are constituted by two overlapping governance triangles: one of recreation-host-customer, the other of preservation-enforcer-violator. Each of these three-sided discourses shifts in competing and overlapping ways, resulting in regulatory projects that are highly contradictory.

The most prominent strategy in attempting to reconcile host/ enforcers who act upon customer/violators is the widespread goal of 'public safety and security,' which is mentioned frequently in mission statements. For example:

> [I]t shall be the intent and purpose of the Division of Parks and Recreation to adopt only those minimal Rules and Regulations that are essential to the protection of Park resources and improvements thereto and to the safety, protection, and general welfare of the visitors ... (Delaware A:s.1.1)

The discourses of 'public safety and security' cast rangers in an overarching role as law-enforcing 'protectors,' while still ostensibly presenting a helpful, tourist-friendly face. This emphasis on safety and security relies on the promotion of a reflexive environment of risk: that visitors are at risk from the 'wild' surroundings of the park as well as from other visitors who are present in the wild environment, and, reflexively, the 'natural' features of the park need to be preserved and protected from people. Both personal and environmental risk are bound together in a way that provides for powerful moral effect: the 'preservation' of nature is linked to questions of personal conduct, and personal safety is linked to the presence of a 'natural,' 'wild' environment. The construction of risk in park missions is located in two intimately related locations that couple and uncouple in programs of public safety and security: the promotion of morally correct personal behaviour, and the morally worthy cause of 'saving' and preserving the environment.

What power and authority do park rangers have in carrying out the contradictions of the preservation/recreation mandates?[12] Even though rangers are initially designated as officers for the purpose of carrying out park legislation, they usually accumulate additional authorities 'on top' of the powers given them at the time of their parks appointment. This 'piggybacking' is possible by virtue of their initial appointment: they become agents of the general category of law to which the park legislation belongs. For example, if park law is a provincial act, they become eligible to enforce all provincial acts (liquor, motor vehicles, trespass) by virtue of their status as 'provincial offences officers' (Ontario A). This piggybacking of authorities is often supported by specific sections in park law that give rangers blanket police powers. These provisions are remarkable in demonstrating how ill-defined and confused ranger programs are in carrying out preservation/recreation mandates. While carefully providing for the appointment of park officers as an alternative to police officers, who might not be sensitive to the needs of nature recreation/preservation, legislators and administrators weaken this intent by providing rangers with sweeping but vague police powers that encourage law enforcer mentalities.

The boundary between police officers and rangers is further blurred by the fact that rangers often receive police- like training; they also carry police weapons, including side arms, pepper spray, mace, and nightsticks, and many drive police-like vehicles. Many ranger programs also utilize police-like ranks and commissions. As parks officers often share concurrent jurisdictions with police, rangers sometimes carry out joint programs with local police forces that are targeting alcohol and drug use. This is especially prevalent in parks that are adjacent to built-up urban areas. The result is that, even though rangers are appointed for the purposes of a specific act, they soon acquire a wide range of authorities based on several pieces of legislation. These allow park rangers to 'hop' from different authority bases and utilize a broad repertoire of power techniques in their encounters with customer-violators. The consequences of this piggybacked ranger authority is that trivial offences such as littering or playing a loud radio can be manipulated within a matrix of authorities and constructed as serious offences deserving of heavy-handed intervention.

Let me provide an example from my own experience as a park warden. I observe someone littering in the park, an offence under Section 3(1) of the regulations of the Provincial Parks Act, which provides for a fine of $103. However, the act provides no arrest, search, or mandatory identification provisions for littering – an appropriate level of authority for such a trivial offence. I decide to charge this person, and ask him for identification. He refuses. At this point, as an officer enforcing the Parks Act, I can do little else. I cannot legally demand identification, nor can I arrest or detain him. He is free to go, and it would be up to me to identify him through other means.

On the other hand, I am not just an officer for the Parks Act, I have other authorities piggybacked onto my parks designation that are deemed necessary to carry out my goals of 'public safety,' such as my authority to enforce liquor, trespass, and motor vehicle legislation. In addition, as the result of case law it has been established that while I am on duty I am a peace officer for the purposes of the Criminal Code, an authority backed by a vague section of the Parks Act that gives me the 'power and authority' of a provincial police officer (Ontario A:s.13). To deal with this violator, I draw on these piggybacked authorities that broaden the range of powers I can exercise. I could jump laterally into other provincial acts that have arrest or identification provisions (Have you been drinking, Sir?), or I could provoke him into breaking a provision of one of these acts (Did you just use insulting language, sir?). I could also 'jump up' into the Criminal Code, using the encounter to invoke my status as a peace officer; he is, by not providing me with identification, 'obstructing a peace officer' or engaging in 'public mischief,' both arrestable offences. As my powers snowball, the event itself may be re-formed to justify my actions: in extreme circumstances the offender could be charged with several criminal offences while the littering charge was forgotten. In most cases, however, I would never intend to lay charges. It is enough that I have coerced or intimidated the 'offender' into doing what I want, and, knowing that if there is any question about my behaviour (i.e., no right to arrest or demand identification), I can justify my actions within this matrix of piggybacked authorities which support a repertoire of coercive techniques.

Rangers offer a vivid example of how the efforts of legislators to create specific agents with limited 'powers' as an alternative to police enforcement are often undermined: once given an authority base, agents can piggyback authorities through the nature of administrative appointments, often by adopting programs of 'public safety' and 'public service' that are rationalized by park missions that emphasize both recreation and preservation. Once enabled by park legislation, park rangers accumulate a wide range of authorized powers that can be easily used in arbitrary ways to construct and capture the park user within a detailed regime of order and permission.[13]

The Securing of Compliance

I conclude this chapter by focusing on how the widespread goal of compliance to preservation/recreation missions constructs a notion of permission that is peculiar to emparkment order. For example, in Michigan (C): 'It is the duty of the employee to make clear to the public the reason for our rules and regulations, gaining respect and compliance through tact, sensitivity and knowledge, rather than threats of arrest and court action.' The deployment of the notion of compliance by park authorities is significant because it marks a shift from the enforcement of specific, situational rules of conduct to the securing of a state of subjectivity through the management of a population of park users.[14] Enforcement is 'done' to an individual, compliance is a condition that is secured in a population. Compliance is gained 'voluntarily' (Washington C:2) 'at the lowest possible level of enforcement' (Georgia B:1, E); it is a quality that is 'ensured' (Georgia C:3) and 'encouraged' (Alberta J:2), something that rangers 'inform and seek' (Massachusetts C), often with 'materials designed to educate visitors' (British Columbia C) or through other efforts of 'education and coercion' (Massachusetts B:9).

The 'gentle way' of compliance is supported by Neighbourhood Watch and other community policing-type initiatives. These efforts range from citizens acting as 'campground hosts' who help register campers and give them advice on park regulations, to schemes where the public can 'report an offender' such as a poacher or litterbug. The form of volunteerism exhibited in these programs is highly congruent with the moral tone of park missions, which promote an abdication of personal need for the 'greater good' of the environment. The growing role of community policing technology in traditional police forces mirrors this 'host' mentality in parks.

Compliance represents an effort to secure a general condition of self-regulating discipline, in contrast to situational threats 'of arrest and court action' that characterize 'law enforcement.' Implicit in the goal of compliance is self-regulation – it seems redundant to talk of self compliance – 'that only' the individual him- or herself can agree to comply, can enter into a voluntary state of obedience and conformity.[15] Park visitors are expected, by the very fact of their entering into a park, to be compliant to emparkment order. 'The privilege of any person,' states a California statute, 'to be present in any unit under control of the Department of Parks and Recreation is hereby expressly conditioned upon compliance by that person with all applicable laws and regulations' (California B:s.4300).[16]

The securing of compliance requires practices which target the population of park visitors, one of the most prominent being *permitting*, the process of being authorized to go to a designated area of the park and perform a particular recreation after paying a fee. In New Jersey a permit 'means a formal request on forms supplied by the State Park Service, supported by all necessary data requested by reference on the form, for approval of a use, properly executed and signed by personnel of the State Park Service lawfully designated by the Director of the Division of Parks and Forestry' (New Jersey, A: 3). Camping permits are perhaps the most common form which records 'requested' information on individual visitors, their vehicles, equipment, and purpose of their stay. As a legal form, the permit is an important tool for rangers: the cancelling of a permit for regulation-breaking immediately renders the person a 'trespasser' on the campsite and subject to eviction. Permitting most often takes place at official park entry points such as gatehouses and park offices, and self-serve permits have become popular in the off-season or at more remote locations. More specialized permits for 'special permission' are often considered for activities such as rock climbing, cave exploring, or the use of metal detectors.

Permits act to homogenize the particular activity of an individual user into a general framework of aggregate obedience to park order: rule-breaking is seen in the context of an infraction against the general order of the park, against the condition of being compliant to a mission of regulated exploitation. Any particular incident of rule-breaking can be constructed as an act of disobedience against all park laws, a movement nicely captured by a Delaware park manager who listed 'permit compliance violations,' not any particular activity, as a main enforcement problem (Delaware B). Permitting allows for the quantification of visitor activity and the calculation of 'compliance rates for park permits' that are used to analyse 'enforcement performances' (Kansas D:11).[17] This allows park governments to use compliance rates to construct an endless number of projects for themselves, as full compliance is never possible. This may involve focusing on one specific activity (such as the consumption of alcohol) or groups of people (such as 'college kids' during a holiday weekend) who are constructed as a visible compliance problem. As a technology of representation, permitting acts at a distance to construct a notion of authority and permission which can actively be patrolled by emparkment agents. More subtly, permitting constructs a web of permission-driven compliance throughout park space, evoking the park as a permissive whole that is congruent with the notion of an innocent, unrestrictive, 'natural' space.

CHAPTER THREE

Regulating Park Space

What is an ideology without a space to which it refers, a space to which it describes, whose vocabulary and links it makes use of, and whose code it embodies? ... Ideology per se might well be said to consist primarily in a discourse upon social space. (emphasis added)

Henri Lefebvre, *The Production of Space*

The most visible aspect of the mission of regulated exploitation is the ordered appearance of park space. In the public imagination, 'natural' park space stands as a permissive expanse that has escaped the control of civilizing technology, that is an apparent relief from the crowded concrete jungle of urban life. When park visitors arrive at the gates of North American parks, they are about to enter a highly sanitized landscape that is intensely ordered, that tells people where to go, what to do, and how long to do it. The so-called 'wild' space of emparked nature parodies the public expectation that parks should be an exception, not an example, of the ordered regimen of urban life.

This chapter examines how the emparkment mission is operationalized through the ordering of park space, how park space is *designated* through the use of specific technologies that mark and cordon off space into areas where specific conduct is permitted, prohibited, or restricted. I focus on how this ordering of space constructs an experience of bewilderment and path-lessness, a labyrinth that provides an experience of freedom within a regime of emparked wildness.

Designating Permission

In the broadest spatial sense, a park is considered to be a 'wild' and 'natural' public space marked by an external boundary that acts as a 'delineation of state interest' (Oklahoma, A:725:30-2-4). The park boundary dramatizes a threshold that park visitors pass through to enter into the 'wilderness' destination of the park. Park legislation often provides detailed prescriptions for the establishment and maintenance of park boundaries. For example:

> The Office of State Parks shall place and maintain such signs along the boundary of all developed property at intervals of not more than one-eighth mile. Such signs shall face in a direction so as to be visible before entering upon state parks' property ... Such signs shall be placed on trees, posts or other supports at a distance of at least three feet above ground level and not more than 10 feet above ground level. (Louisiana A:333C(c) (d))

This dramatization of the park as a guarded space is carried out in the operation of official, controlled entrances where park visitors are permitted and registered. 'No person shall enter a provincial park by any means,' states a typical statute, 'except at a point designated for the purpose of entry by the superintendent' (Ontario A:s.23). Park entrances often have a majestic quality to them, such as the stone arch at Yellowstone, or the fort-like East Gatehouse of Algonquin. *Permitting* acts not only as a fiscal practice centred around revenue generation, but also ties the conduct of individuals to a specific parcel of space in the park, epitomized by common permissions such as these: 'swimming and wading are permitted in designated areas only' (Nebraska B:s.001.20) and 'camping is permitted only in designated campgrounds' (Iowa A:1).

This binding of space and conduct relies on the legislative practice of *designating*, dividing up park space into marked areas where specific activities are permitted, restricted, or prohibited. Designating configures park space in such a way that the park landscape can be presented as both preserved nature and recreational playspace. The preservation/recreation contradiction of park missions is spatially actualized as a ruled series of sites where marked boundaries empark a 'preserved' nature that can be used for a range of official recreations. Relying on a context of personal and environmental risk so visibly evoked by the ranger, designating is vividly linked to discourses of 'safety and security.' For example, in New Jersey:

> The State Park Service shall designate or direct any and all recreational or other use on its lands and waters and within its facilities to such specific areas or locations within or upon said land, waters, and facilities as will be in the best interest of conservation, recreation, preservation and management of the natural and historic resources and the *health, safety and welfare of all persons concerned.* (New Jersey A:s.7:2-2.2; emphasis added)

Moreover, such discourses can focus on the benefits that designated uses can provide to each individual visitor:

> The Superintendents may regulate activities and uses of each State park in accordance with the designations provided in Regulation .01 ... in order to promote the designated uses for the benefit of each individual. (Maryland A:.02 (D))

How is park space designated? The technique of designating requires that park space be physically marked and cordoned, epitomized by park legislators who define 'designated' as 'indicated by a sign' (Georgia D:s.391-5-2-.02), an area 'signed on the ground' (Michigan E:s.1.2(7)), and to 'indicate, specify, or make recognizable by some mark, sign or name' (California B:s.4303(1)). This act of 'making recognizable' is a widespread power given to park authorities. Two examples:

> A park officer may erect a sign or other device specifying an area in which specific activities are *permitted, prohibited or restricted* in a park or recreation area. (British Columbia B:s.10; emphasis added)

> The Division shall, by posting appropriate signs, regulate the use of food and beverages, including alcoholic beverages, *or other human*

activities as appropriate to protect park property or the enjoyment and safety of other users.[1] (Florida A:s.16D-2.003 (12); emphasis added)

The act of designating park space relies on the use of signage, or 'official graffiti' (Hermer and Hunt 1996), explicitly articulated advisements, watches, warnings, prohibitions, and directions which have the specific effect of constructing self-regulating objects. These powers are often complemented by prohibitions against the defacing or removal of official graffiti. For example, in Louisiana 'it is strictly forbidden to destroy, deface, remove, alter, damage, or disturb any building, sign, marker ...' (Louisiana A:303b). New Jersey state legislators nicely capture the pervasive use of official graffiti in designating park space in their operational definition of 'signs,' which means 'any object, device, display or structure, or part thereof, situated outdoors or indoors, which is used to advertise, identify, instruct, display, direct, or attract attention to an object, person, institution, organization, business, product, service, event or location by any means, including words, letters, figures, designs, symbols, fixtures, colors, illumination or projected images'[2] (New Jersey A:s.7:2-1.7).

Park governments administer the posting of official graffiti through the use of sign manuals and design guides. Sign manuals act as 'communication instruments' (Parks Canada B) to field staff, and are products of an extensive network that approves and catalogues a lexicon of official graffiti. Park sign systems act to 'identify, direct, warn, or regulate' (Parks Canada B) in a way that provides for 'economy of manufacture, ease of installation and minimal maintenance' (Minnesota D:1). While textual and iconic qualities of sign messages are a major concern of sign manuals, park technicians rely on the fact that the public has already been exposed to a wide range of internationally recognized symbols (Utah K:2-20). A sign must 'command attention' and 'demand respect of the user' and 'give adequate time for proper response' by exhibiting 'continuity, legibility and utility' (Minnesota D:1). Sign colours such as 'mission brown' (Vermont C:1) and yellow are recommended, because they 'blend aesthetically to most surrounding seasonal colour situations' (Minnesota D; Washington E:3).

A primary concern of sign manual writers is to check the often impulsive character of field staff who seemingly erect signage at every possible opportunity. Park staff can only erect 'home-made signs' in emergency conditions, otherwise staff are expected to request signs through official channels. Sign manuals stress to field staff that signs are to be used conservatively; this is especially true for inscriptions that attempt to order personal conduct. 'In requesting any sign,' states a Vermont manual, 'consideration must be given to need. Is the sign really needed, or is it a response to an isolated problem that can be handled without adding another sign. One should be careful that too many signs are not used, becoming detrimental to both the visitor's enjoyment and the operation of the park' (Vermont C:1).

Signs are considered an integral part of the presentation of the authority of the government to empark natural surroundings; they also signify the 'corporate identity' of park government (Parks Canada B). 'Aside from providing information,' states a Minnesota manual, 'signs become department signatures and convey the tone for the area before the threshold is even crossed by the visitor. Sign content directly influences the user's impressions ... Improper terminology, conflicting messages, grammatical errors, inappropriateness of color combinations, and bad location inhibit the signs' effectiveness and can be dangerous. Such misuse of signs can result in disrespect at those locations where signs are needed' (Minnesota D:8). Signs also play a crucial role in the liminal character of park space, setting a 'tone' and preparing park users to cross the thresholds of designated space. This emphasis on disrespect expressed by the Minnesota manual writer is especially remarkable: park signs are expected to engender respect for the natural environment at the very location where a sign evokes the presence of human intervention.

Sign manuals typically make distinctions between regulatory signs that govern situational conduct, and informational or directional signage that assists in reaching a destination. Manuals suggest that conduct signage should be located at the specific place

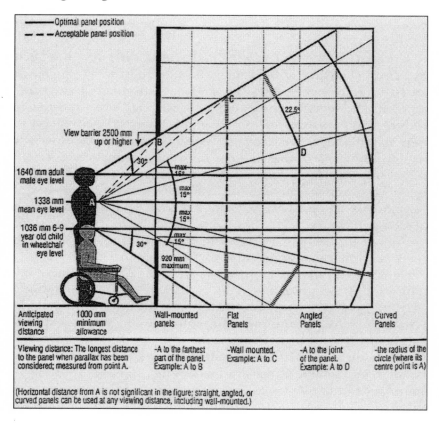

Figure 2 Viewing angles and distances for signage (Courtesy of Parks Canada)

where conduct is to be ordered, while directional and informational signage should be erected along predetermined routes through which park visitors will travel. Signage should be posted within the 'sight line' (Vermont C) of the park visitor, within the viewers' 'cone of vision' (Washington E:II-4). Park staff are instructed to erect signs at right angles to the direction of visitor travel, except in the case of reflective signs, which should be turned slightly away so that their legibility is not obscured by the reflection (Washington E:II-5). Signs for pedestrians or 'very slow traffic' can be placed on short posts to be 'readily seen,' while signs for vehicular traffic must be placed in a zone of vision which allows the reader to 'intake' a sign's message and have time to respond (Minnesota D:10). As illustrated in Figure 2, park cartographers are able to calculate the optimum placement of the sign face or 'panel' surface in relation to a range of 'eye level' positions.

Official graffiti constructs an emparkment gaze which attempts to capture and control the velocity of bodies through the act of reading or 'intaking' inscriptions. The flow of visitors and cars itself becomes an object which is governed as part of the temporal character of each 'wild' place. This temporal ordering relies on the use of cartographic models which can precisely act 'at a distance' and project the designated experience of park visitors through the use of sign plans that carry out a 'sequencing of signs' as depicted in Figure 3.

Visitors travelling along specific predetermined routes can be controlled through the use of 'confirming' and 'reassurance' markers along such routes (Washington E:S.3-5), a technique commonly used in theme parks to visually chaperone the visitor from attraction to attraction (Wylson and Wylson 1994). The use of networks of signs allows park managers to intentionally construct the impression of a complex and integrated environment within which people are not immediately able to take their 'cue' from the surrounding area (see Parks Canada B:58). This construction of spontaneity and complexity evokes an atmosphere of disorder within which park users are prompted to look to official inscriptions to navigate their way.

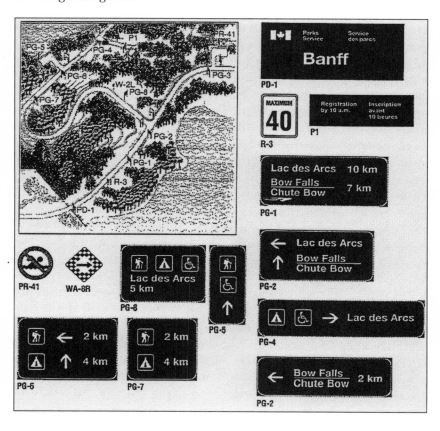

Figure 3 Sequencing of informational or directional signage (Courtesy of Parks Canada)

The expectation of personal and environmental risk evoked by designated space is most visibly carried out by the use of official graffiti. A 'do not feed the bear' sign evokes the presence of wild (and possibly hungry) bears, 'a moose crossing' sign suggests both the possibility of seeing a moose and of hitting one with your car, the 'no littering' sign evokes the specter of pollution and re-enforces the morally correct trait of cleanliness, impelling one to 'save the environment.' The use of official graffiti often generates a dilemma for park managers: should park visitors who visit the park expecting a dangerous 'wild' landscape be protected from every possible hazard, even those that are human-made? There is a striking paradox for park managers in the use of signage which acts to warn visitors that a particular site or activity is dangerous, an admission that places a burden of liability on the park to ensure that a potentially hazardous site or conduct is policed. This dilemma is especially ironic considering that one of the attractive features of signage is its ability to construct a population of self-regulating park users who do not need to be actively policed by park staff.

Field staff are often warned of the issues of liability in using signage to regulate potentially dangerous situations. For example, in Minnesota, an assistant state attorney advised park staff: 'If a natural condition exists which could be dangerous in some cir-cumstances, such as a steep hill or strange fungi in the water which causes rashes, it would probably be a good idea to post signs stating, in the first instance (steep hill), and in the second in-stance either (no swimming) or (swimmer's itch area – swim at your own risk). I don't think that signs should be posted prohibit-ing certain activities; if the prohibition is not enforced, it makes for greater liability if someone is injured engaged in such activity' (Minnesota D:10).

Certainly, there seems to be almost unlimited scope for park managers to construct park features that will look like a 'natural condition' by virtue of the fact that an almost endless number of hazards (e.g., steep hills) can be posed as dangers to the park visitor. The use of official graffiti as insurance against liability must be carefully managed if the prohibited conduct is not actively policed (e.g., NO Swimming). Ideally, liability should remain at the self-regulating discretion of the park user (Swim at your own risk).

As depicted in Figure 4, official graffiti can be used to regulate almost any conduct that can be depicted in the form of a pictogram. The type of recreational uses officially permitted by park authorities and designated with official graffiti goes well beyond simple picnicking and sunbathing to include a stunning array of recreational pursuits. For example Wisconsin State Park legislation lists the following 'permitted recreational uses': 'cross-country skiing, birdwatching, dog sledding, dog training, dog trials, falconry, foot racing, hang-gliding, hiking, horseback riding competitions, hot air ballooning, hunting, land sailing, model aircraft flying, model rocket flying, nature study, Scouting jamborees, skydiving, sleigh riding, snowmobiling, steeplechase events, trail biking, trapping' (Wisconsin A:s.18(b, j)). However, any activity or object can be constituted and then slashed out of existence by the standardized 'prohibition slash' or 'tick' superimposed on any activity initially constructed within a framework of permission (Hermer and Hunt 1996).

A major goal of the designating of park space is to enforce a segregation between 'day use' areas and the 'night use' areas that facilitate camping. This segregation – which forms a major theme in the ordering of conduct – provides for even tighter control and surveillance of those who wish to erect shelters and sleep in the park overnight.

As Figure 5 illustrates, the spatial arrangement of organized campgrounds ironically mimics the design of North American suburbs: numbered and posted campsite lots, side by side facing a road, arranged in avenues and boulevards that conveniently access utilities such as water and electricity. The typical camp *site* is further arranged into designated places: typically, a parking pad for the car, a fireplace, a picnic table, and a pad for the tent. This arrangement echoes the structure of a suburban home: the garage, kitchen, family dining room, and bedroom which sit on a numbered lot. The construction of the campsite as a 'living area' (see Figure 6) is a good example of how, within designated space,

Figure 4 Symbols used for State Park System signs (Courtesy of the Oklahoma Division of State Parks)

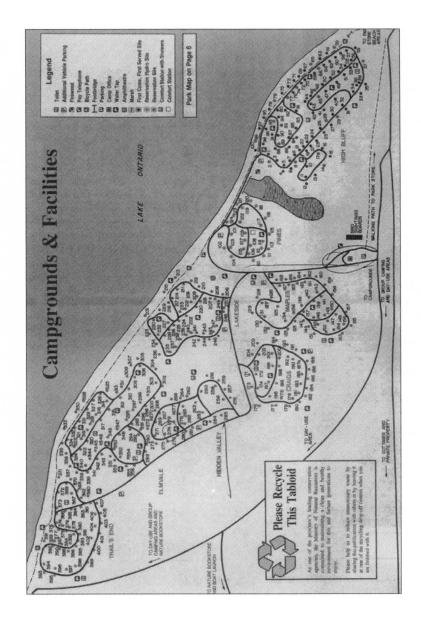

Figure 5 Map of Presqu'ile Provincial Park campground (Courtesy of the Ontario Ministry of Natural Resources)

everything, including social actors, are 'figured' in 'their place.' Even so-called primitive or interior campsites are informally laid out to mimic this domestic arrangement.

While park space is primarily designated in ways that tie specific parcels of space to visitor conduct that is permitted, restricted, or prohibited, there is what I will call a *secondary* form of designating which classifies park space into categories of *relative* naturalness or wildness. Often explicitly done within programs of 'park classification' initiated in the 1960s (Killan 1993), this designating often classifies the park itself – certain zones of the park, trails, campgrounds, and so on – into categories that express 'natural,' 'cultural,' or 'historic' values.[3] This secondary designating is useful to park governments because it overlays the space permitted to carry out preservation/recreation missions with an overarching designation that re-codes and re-states the park or park features as 'natural' and 'wild.' South Dakota offers a graphic example in the secondary designating of its campgrounds, which have generated the following classifications:

- Modern: a campground equipped with flush toilets, lavatories, hot showers, and individual camping pads
- Semi-modern: a campground equipped with individual camping pads and with flush toilets, but without showers or a shower house and vault toilets
- Basic: a campground equipped with vault toilets where camping is allowed on camping pads, grassed areas, or parking lots[4] (South Dakota A:s.41:03:04:01)

Other examples include Iowa, where the terms 'modern area' and 'non-modern area' are used to specify the lack of flush toilets and showers, and Washington, which uses the term 'primitive campsite' to describe a campsite which 'may not have any of the amenities of a 'standard site' which 'is served by nearby domestic water, sink waste, garbage disposal, and flush comfort station' (Washington B:s.WAC 352-32-010). The primary designation of an area where organized camping is permitted, an activity that epitomizes regulated exploitation, is recast in the secondary des-

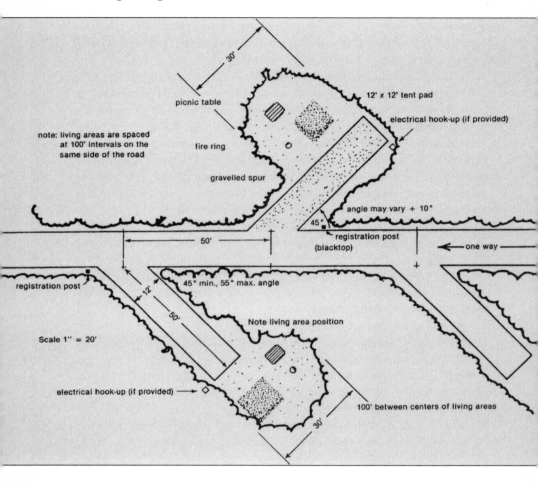

Figure 6 Typical campsite layout (Courtesy of the Wisconsin Department of Natural Resources)

ignating as being 'wild' and 'natural' by evoking the powerful contexts of 'modernity' and 'primitiveness.' This effort to make the built environment of the park appear natural through secondary designating is often accompanied by prescriptions having to do with building appearance. For example, 'Building architecture is to be compatible with the pastoral environment,' states a Nebraska policy, 'rustic in nature, harmoniously colored and have non-reflective roofs and sidings' (Nebraska D:s.001.26H2).

The fact that the 'natural' state of campgrounds is defined in terms of amenities that serve personal hygiene is especially notable. Quite remarkably, not having access to a shower or flush toilet makes one campsite more 'primitive,' 'non-modern,' and 'natural' then another. Secondary forms of designating are perhaps the most vivid expression of the linkage between personal hygiene and the perceived disorder of a natural landscape. Refraining from a shower for a week on an interior camping trip is evoked as a wilderness experience, regardless of the actual ecological qualities of the landscape.

Underlying these descriptions specifically, and the designation of space generally, is the idea that nature has been corrupted by 'modernity,' that parks offer a pre-modern or less modern place that is more 'pure' and 'innocent.' Certainly, the casting of the past as a more innocent time against which a more corrupt present can be compared is a central characteristic of a broad range of discourses of moral regulation. As depicted in Figure 7, the practice of designating space, through the deployment of official graffiti, represents nature as an object that is knowable, recognizable, and identifiable. There are no 'natural' spaces or objects that cannot be homogenized in the categorized catalogue of resource management and charted with icons and texts on the two-dimensional surface of a map or 'master plan.' All park space can be ruled by immutable mobiles, can be inscribed and configured to represent nature as a visible collection of recreational objects and spaces.

As Figure 7 so vividly illustrates, to designate is to classify space and create a grid of relativity where every object of cordoned space depends on the location of every other object. Tom Markus

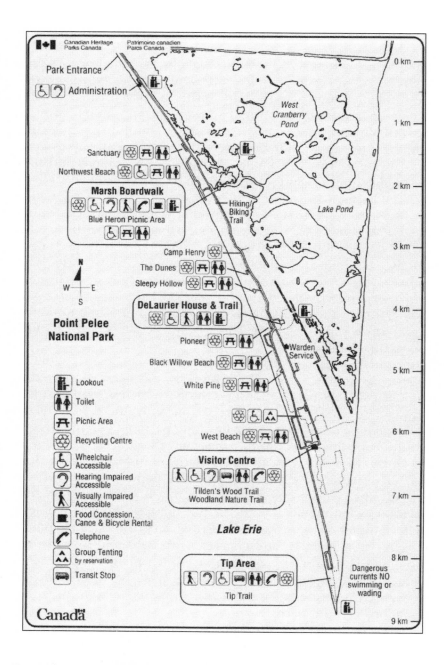

Figure 7 Map of Point Pelee National Park (Courtesy of Parks Canada)

(1993) has described this form of spatialization as constituting a 'syntax of nextness.' Park space, as a *class* of designated spaces and objects, creates an interlocked landscape where the maintenance of order depends upon the enforcement of all boundaries of designation. These boundaries construct park visitors as transient subjects that pass through the ostensibly wild landscape of the park that is represented as being permanent.

The designation of park space, carried out through the deployment of two-dimensional texts by the official graffitists of park government, has the effect of reorganizing park space as a fillable volume, as a set of containers that can be filled to a predetermined capacity or limit. This quality is often expressed in park planning literature that describes the 'carrying capacity' or 'public use limit,' where designated space can only support a set 'volume' of recreational activities measured in terms of numbers of people, cars, cottages, boats, and so on. For example, 'The Assistant Secretary shall, upon recommendation of the unit manager, approve a carrying capacity for each state park area. Once a carrying capacity has been reached, or when additional visitors would adversely impact the park, the unit manager is authorized to close the park site to incoming visitors' (Louisiana A:303 (E)).[5] This containerization of park space spatializes a *permanent transience* where park space is 'filled' and 'emptied' of park visitors under a schedule that is enforced through the issuance and circulation of permits. This permanent transience works to manage, direct, and authorize park visitor experience, which is constantly framed within the order of designated space. Official graffiti is not simply emblematic of what is restricted, permitted, and prohibited, but represents a catalogue of 'natural' experiences that is authorized by the absent experts of park government.

The Labyrinth

The most specialized form of designated space is the trail, a space that fuses together notions of both personal and environmental risk within a powerful moral ethos. Trails are considered to be a 'mechanism' (Parks Canada C) which carries out the contradictory mission of emparked nature – that people can recreate in a natural environment in a way that will preserve nature. At first glance, trails seem to be arbitrary expressions of wandering, routes that have been worn by those who have 'found their way' through. In fact, from recreational trails that provide a twenty-minute walk, to elaborate state or national trails that follow some historical or ecological route, trails are landscaped by a detailed and highly technical regime. A recent trend in park making has been the emparkment of abandoned railway tracks as state trails, often referred to as 'linear parks.'

Trail manuals and design guides provide detailed prescriptions about the layout, construction, and maintenance of park trails. Trail technicians stress the importance of building trails that provide 'scenic interest' through the integration of 'strong spatial or visual characteristics.' Trails are intentionally designed to meander and have an arbitrary, unplanned look to them. Trail makers are encouraged to utilize various 'loop' and 'maze like' routes, and be curvilinear because 'twists and turns provide interest' (Parks Canada C). Trail elevation should be manipulated – often with the use of built platforms and stands – to provide viewers with vistas of park geography. Prominent natural features such as a waterfall or an old tree can provide a presentational node around which a trail can meander. Audible features also should be integrated into trail experience, such as the sound of running water, or wind through a tree canopy. Water forms are considered to be an especially valuable presentational feature, as they provide for the image, sound, and possible 'feel' of something natural. A Newfoundland and Labrador manual (E:25) describes the ideal way a trail should approach a waterfall: 'Trail users are first given a view of a waterfall from a distance. The trail is diverted away from this view until further along when the waterfall is seen more closely at a different angle. Variety and anticipation together heighten interest.'

Trails wander around objects of interest, exposing the view from different levels and elevations, faking an impression of distance. Trail designers, while constructing an experience of variety, anticipation, and surprise, also have to make sure that users are not overly challenged or taxed, and that they have a comfortable experience. Trail grades must be carefully calculated – a sustained grade of anything more than 20 per cent is unacceptable (Parks Canada C). The tread of the trail is also given some detail in trail manuals, most notably because of the opportunity for trail makers to increase the 'carrying capacity' of the trail by providing for an especially durable surfacing. Perhaps even more important, such techniques allow park managers to reduce the visual impact of heavy use, and maximize what Walters (1982:296) has referred to as the 'perceptual carrying capacity' of the trail. Woodchips are an especially popular trail cover because of their 'natural' appearance, and the fact that chips can be produced as part of the cleanup after the trail has been blazed. Trail manuals frequently prescribe the height and width to which trails should be maintained and the line of sight within which signs should be used; they also emphasize the importance of keeping particular vistas open for the public to see. Trails make frequent use of official graffiti, not just to chaperone the user along the trail, but also to provide texts that 'interpret' nature. For example, in Florida a trail label entitled 'Life from the Dead' reads: 'Even after death, trees abound with other forms of life. Bacteria are decomposing the plant tissues. Termites, woodboring beetles and carpenter ants are feeding within. These are eaten by woodpeckers, lizards, toads and shrews. The web of life will, in time, reduce this tree to a rich brown area of humus on the forest floor – waiting to be used by other living things' (Florida C:18).

The evocation of this 'web of life,' which is constantly evoked in park experience, constructs the park users as part of a 'living system' that can be experienced. The trail itself, looping and inverting through this wild atmosphere, only to return to the beginning, becomes a metaphor itself for the natural cycle of nature. These interpretive trails, often referred to as 'self-guiding' trails, are posted with official graffiti which informs, guides, warns, and advises the hiker in a context of both personal and environmental risk.[6] The effect of such texts is to direct the gaze of the visitor to experience what the park 'nature interpreter' has deemed wild, a construction that often evokes the past and future as part

of the construction of a natural present: park landscape is depicted as wild because of what it once was, ('a virgin forest' or 'a
glacier route') or what it will be ('a mature oak forest' or 'an
etched canyon'). Often these texts draw on evolutionary tropes
that point out 'stages' of ecological development, creating the
effect that the park itself is simply a stage in a 'natural' park
ecology. The directing of the park user's gaze has the effect of
inserting designated park spaces as benign parts of the natural
history of the landscape. The paradigm example is the 'tree ring'
display, where a tree disk is displayed exhibiting its rings with the
decades of growth and dendro-climatic features such as hail storms,
lightening strikes, and sunspots marked with calendar years. Often the 'birthday' of the park is noted on the ring-year as if it were
some sort of natural occurrence that happened to the tree! Nature is depicted as an expression of incremental distances that
proceed towards some logical end. Such common spectacles depict nature as an object that can be 'split open' and read in a
linear, evolutionary way.

Designated park space is constructed as being pathless and
disordered, as a wilderness where one can enter, find one's way
through, and depart, all without leaving any sign of one's presence. This *manufactured pathlessness* is vividly illustrated in widespread programs featuring 'no trace camping' where you can
'keep others from knowing you were there,' where you can travel
'through wilderness ... leaving only the temporary imprint of your
footsteps [which] may at first seem impossible. But such is not the
case. There are simple and easy ways to leave Yukon wilderness the
way it was before you arrived – sometimes even better. Much is just
common sense' (Yukon A).

Note the ongoing emphasis on how human presence can im-
prove what is already wild, leaving it 'sometimes even better.' But
the possibility of leaving only your temporary footprint is indeed
impossible. The brochure advises a few paragraphs later that 'It's
best to stay on an existing trail if possible. The impact has already
happened. But if the trail is one used by wildlife, be alert! Otherwise you may be an unwelcome surprise for the bear around the
next corner. Watch for tracks and make noise, especially if travel-

ling in dense bush, near noisy streams, around corners, over hills, or upwind' (Yukon A).

This 'pathless wilderness' clearly requires paths, even if they happen to be on a trail 'used by wildlife' – a ridiculous notion that suggests humans are just another species of animal travelling through the wild surroundings. This passage nicely illustrates how a path constantly evokes 'wild risk,' that you never know what lies 'around the corner' or 'over the hill,' risk evoking features of trails that park managers intentionally construct to provide an experience of wandering and danger.

A vivid example of the self-regulated experience of trail space is the use of lookout trails, or observation points, often located on viewing platforms and elevated sites. These self-guided lookouts feature a panorama, an unbroken view of the landscape that creates a spectacle of sunsets and sunrises, of horizons that evoke the wilderness quality of endless expanses that appear untouched by human activity.[7] This effect, which practices a visual synecdoche where the view framed by the perspective of the lookout is made to stand for the whole park, acts to enforce the image of nature as permanent, while evoking the presence of humans as temporary and unharmful. The enforcement of this transience is integral to the manufacturing of the natural: humans are present in park space only temporarily, they can tread in the wilderness only momentarily. Human presence is transient, fleeting, unharmful.

The moral metaphor of the path which is so powerfully evoked by park trails suggests the possibility of getting lost, of losing one's way both physically and psychologically, of being in a state of be*wild*erment. The connection between the 'path' and the dangers of being lost are also vividly evoked in the famous nursery tale about Hansel and Gretel, who are abandoned deep in the forest and left to die, their only hope of getting home dashed after a trail of breadcrumbs carefully dropped behind them had been eaten by Ravens.[8]

The manipulation of space through practices of designating creates an expectation of disorder, of an environment that is considered wild because it is perceived as dangerous. The natural spaces of parks offer the experience of a labyrinth, a contrived state of complexity and bewilderment where one can only find one's way out with a guidance system. The labyrinthine character of park space is absolutely key to the construction of parks users as self-regulating objects who must constantly face risk. As I have discussed above, with the example of the use of park signage to 'prompt' parks visitors, park experience is always within the framework of guidance – visitors are never really on their own. This is as true for an organized campground as it is for a remote forested area. Emparked space is a series of destinations within destinations, a sequence or series of recurring thresholds, a geography of liminality (Shields 1991; Zukin 1991:213). The pathlesness of trails becomes a peculiar pedagogical tool, where the 'experiential presentation' of wandering on a trail mimics the construction of an image of nature as a cyclic system where death and life sustain one another.

The labyrinthine order of park space constructs an experience which collapses space and time, producing a particular temporal aspect of emparked nature. While spatial regulation constantly evokes the cyclic, rhythmic character of nature, park space is overlaid with a regime of a linear time discipline ordered by the notion of duration, of the prescribed presence of park visitors who are authorized by permits. The 'emparkment time' is inherently contradictory, where the notion of recycling can only exist when complemented by a notion of linearity which posits future growth and further consumption. As Van Loon and Sabelis argue (1997:297), this contradiction of cyclicity and linearity is central to the construction of the waste management mentalities of late modernity.

The temporal order of park space creates an effect of distance, of travelling somewhere, an allusion of memory and remembrance of a natural past that has been preserved. Even the crossing of a stream, an experience that appears spontaneous and risky, is choreographed by trail designers. As illustrated in Figure 8, each carefully placed stone must be heavy enough to provide a strong foothold in the current, but small enough to provide a challenge to the hiker who must carefully negotiate each step to

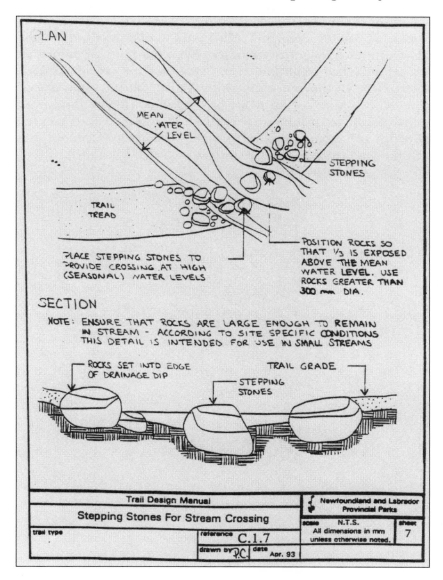

Figure 8 Stepping Stones for Stream Crossing plan (Courtesy of the Department of Tourism and Culture, Government of Newfoundland and Labrador)

reach the safety of the continuing trail. In his discussion of cityscapes, Walter Benjamin (1979) drew our attention to the labyrinthine character of memory with a conceptualization that seems even more applicable to emparked nature (see also Gilloch 1996:67–8). To move in a labyrinth is to revisit the same places, while still moving to the heart of something, to 'be lost,' even momentarily, yet still be on a route to discovery. The permitted labyrinth of emparkment offers an experience of freedom, but only through the most precise and exact ordering of the self.

CHAPTER FOUR

The Regulation of Conduct

Consider other state park users. Boisterous, immoral, or indecent conduct will not be tolerated.

Pennsylvania State Area Rules and Regulations

Here I catalogue in some detail how the mission of regulated exploitation is carried out through extensive and sustained discourses of moral order that target the conduct of park visitors. I begin by discussing how park government segregates and prescribes day and night conduct through the tight control of what constitutes 'camping' and 'shelter.' I examine the three main regulatory themes that are framed by this distinction: the keeping of peace and quiet through the regulation of both visual and audible noise, the promotion of decency through the prohibition of public acts of sex and nakedness, and the prescriptions for hygiene and sanitation that ensure a state of cleanliness. The enforcement of these three themes underpins the idealized image of nature represented by park government: a landscape where the 'wild' qualities of 'nature' are manufactured by the promotion of quietness, decency, and hygiene. I focus on how these regulatory themes are simultaneously present in specific regulatory campaigns that target the use of fire and the consumption of alcohol. I conclude by examining how the severe ordering of conduct through a nexus of permissions, restrictions, and prohibitions manufactures a 'natural' environment, a construction that relies on the dramatization of both personal and environmental risk.

Conducting Day and Night

There is a widespread and sustained discursive concern in park legislation about maintaining the distinction between recreational activities, between those that are carried out in the day and those that are carried out at night and centre around 'sleeping over' in the park darkness. This concern is most visibly expressed in the designating of 'day use' areas which are segregated from campgrounds, spaces exclusively set aside for overnight shelter. This detailed distinction is represented most vividly in the extensive pre-scriptions of what constitutes 'camping' and 'shelter.' For exam-ple, 'Camping is defined as the temporary lodging out-of-doors for outdoor recreational purposes and presupposes occupancy of a shel-ter designed for such purpose (i.e., sleeping bag, tent, trailer or other recreational vehicle)' (Nebraska B:s.001.05A).[1] And, '"Camp-ing" means the erecting of a tent or shelter of natural or man-made material, or placing a sleeping bag or other bedding material on the ground or parking a motor vehicle, motor home or trailer for the apparent purpose of overnight occupancy' (Iowa A:3).

Any activity where one can shelter or bed down, conceal or cover one's body, even in or under a sleeping bag or blanket, is considered a sheltering that can occur only on designated camp-sites. Conversely, these definitions are complemented by the pro-hibitions against the use of any sort of 'shelter' in day use areas. Even sunbathers who want a little shade are not exempt, as this Florida regulation illustrates:

> No individual shall erect, maintain, use, or occupy on or in any beach or bathing area any tent, shelter or structure of any kind unless there shall be an unobstructed view into such structure from at least two sides. (Florida A:s.16D-2.004 (2)(d))

Park user conduct is rendered visible at all times, open to inspection by park agents and other users, exposed to being scrutinized as part of the proper order of designated space. Dis-cernible in these regulations is a tone of panic, that within day use space, people might hide their bodies from public view and en-

gage in some sort of unseemly behaviour. This legislative obses-
sion with keeping the body visible and watchable illustrates one of
the most visual paradoxes of park space: parks are attractive as a
'natural' destination because they are perceived as being shel-
tered places where one can 'get away,' yet park space is configured
so that visitor conduct is continually under surveillance and subject to regulatory intervention at any time. This surveillance is
made even more intense through the use of permits which must
be displayed or produced for inspection at all times. Such a system
of permitting evokes the dangerous presence of the unpermitted
person, the stranger who is a risk to other visitors and the 'natural'
environment of the park.

People enter into the 'permissive,' 'free,' and thus 'natural'
space of the park, only to find that they must retreat into the
precarious privacy of their tents to enjoy any measure of freedom.
Park regulators exert an even tighter grip on those who take cover
under shelter at night, by placing restrictions on the type of
people that can sleep over. For example, the state of Montana
asserts that 'a "camper unit" is defined as a motorized vehicle,
motorhome, camping bus, pull-type camper, tent, or any device
designed for sleeping, including a combination of any two that
are used by parents and their unmarried children' (Montana A:
s.A (a)). The literature in fact leaves little doubt that widespread
restrictions on the number and type of people allowed on a site –
in this case as part of a 'camper unit' – are directly linked to the
promotion of the traditional heterosexual family as an additional
control on those who 'camp over.' Campsites are typically restricted to a maximum of five or six unrelated persons; exceptions
are routinely made for families comprising more then six people.
For example, 'campsite occupancy is limited to one family unit
per night or a non family unit not to exceed 6 persons ... A family
unit is composed of members of an immediate family group:
husband, wife, and/or children' (Louisiana A:s.311(f)).

This promotion of 'family unit' camping is complemented by
restrictions on 'non-family unit' overnight guests, as well as on the
number and type of shelter equipment allowed.[2] Widespread
restrictions limiting the pieces of shelter equipment on each

campsite have the effect of restricting the number of 'private' places erected on the site; the implication is that the privacy provided by temporary shelter is best situated within the patriarchal control of the traditional family.[3] This regulatory modelling is even more explicit in regulations that require a camping group to designate a 'head' who is responsible for conduct on the campsite.[4] Thus, campsites take on a suburban character not just in their spatial layout, but also in their promotion of a traditional patriarchal family as an ideal model of disciplinary control for behaviour that takes place behind the 'closed doors' of the tent, hidden from public scrutiny, in the privacy of temporary shelter.

Peace and Quiet

The maintenance of peace and quiet is by far the most prominent topos in the governance of park conduct. While the enforcement of a peaceful public sphere has long been a common law goal of 'good government,' this emphasis takes on a special quality in park governance as peace and quiet are seen as qualities inherent to nature, qualities that should be protected from the din and noise of urban life. Park government considers noisy behaviour that pollutes the 'peace and quiet' of the park not just an offence against the natural environment, but a behaviour that impairs the ability of people to appreciate the quiet and peaceful aspects of nature, a sentiment captured nicely by Alberta park officials, who use the term 'depreciative behaviour' to describe undesirable conduct.[5]

As one would expect, park regulations include prohibitions such as: 'It shall be unlawful to incite or participate in riots, indulge in boisterous, abusive, threatening, indecent or disorderly conduct in any state park area' (Alabama A:s.220-5-.07).[6] While worry about riots in park areas is infrequent, prohibitions against the more subtle forms of disorder are not, especially prohibitions concerning the *appearance* of disorder and the *pretext* or *possibility* of violence – behaviour that can be considered a visual form of 'noise.' As a threat to peacefulness, visual noise is often described as behaviour that causes concern, alarm, discomfort, or fear among park users; like audible noise, it involves conduct that draws attention to itself as behaviour that is 'out of place.' A Massachusetts statute provides a vivid example of visual noise:

> No person shall engage in rough play, pushing, shoving, fighting or games which, *due to the location or nature of the activity,* may cause or tend to cause discomfort, fear or injury to any person or property within the confines of any Division Forest, Park. (Massachusetts As.-304 CMR 12.12; emphasis added)

Certainly, the prohibition of visual noise which may 'tend to cause discomfort' is so broad and capricious it could prohibit any sort of behaviour carried out in public space that might make anyone uncomfortable in any way. We can think then of how the simple presence of certain groups can create 'visual noise' and automatically present a form of disorder that likely would be targeted by authorities; certainly, congregations of teenagers are automatically targeted as probable sources of visual noise that will offend park visitors looking for the peaceful quiet of family camping.

Closely joined to visual noise, which disrupts the appearance of peacefulness, is audible noise, which assaults what was previously quiet. The most common forms of disorderly sound targeted by regulators are generated from what the legislation calls 'noise producing machines,' 'noise making instruments,' 'audio devices' and 'noise producing devices,' which include 'radios,' 'television sets,' 'musical instruments,' 'generators,' 'public address systems,' the 'motorized toy,' the 'motor vehicle,' the 'boombox,' and a 'horn other than a reasonable warning signal' (Tennessee A:s.0400-2-2-.03; Oregon A:s.736-10-045; Wisconsin A:s.3 (1)).[7] Prohibitions targeting these 'noise machines' concern themselves with the volume of noise that offends against the 'right to quiet' as enforced, for example, in Alberta provincial parks (Alberta J: 136). Additionally, there are occasional efforts to establish 'radio free' zones in parks that completely ban the use of all 'noise producing machines.'[8]

A second, closely related form of audible noise targeted by park agents is any language that is considered profane or obscene. For example, in Ontario, 'No person shall use abusive or insulting language within ... a provincial park' (Ontario B:s.7(1)). Additionally, park regulators concern themselves with sounds that simply imply human behaviour that is offensive, especially when it evokes activities that are considered to be of a private nature. These sounds, characterized in the literature as 'loud and unseemly noises,' 'unreasonably harsh sounds,' 'an offensively coarse utterance' (Tennessee A:s.0400-2-2-.07) seem to be directed at noises produced by sexually active bodies. The governance of these different forms of 'noise' provides an opportunity to explore how park legislation constructs the presence of an imaginary person who can be easily offended. Park law must reflexively construct a subject, a personage who is somehow wronged – offended, made uncomfortable, inconvenienced, endangered, and so on – by behaviour that can then be constituted as disorderly. We may take an Oklahoma State Park regulation as an exemplar of this construction:

> Operating equipment or machinery such as an electric generating plant, motor vehicle, audio device or musical instrument which generates unreasonable noise, considering the nature and purpose of the conduct, location, time of day or night, purpose for which the area was established, impact upon park visitors, and other factors that *would govern the conduct of a reasonably prudent* person under such circumstances is prohibited. (Oklahoma A:s.725:30-4-6(a); emphasis added)[9]

Thus, such prohibitions rely on the deployment of a discursive sensibility, embodied most often by a 'reasonably prudent person' who lurks everywhere in the designated geography of park space. This discursive personage not only has an unassailable moral character and a reasonableness against which unreasonable conduct can be constructed, but he or she has a sensibility that can be harmed, offended, annoyed, alarmed, and disturbed at the activities of park visitors.

For example, a New Jersey statute posits a discursive sensibility in the form of visitors who can be offended by 'depreciative behaviour':

> A person shall not engage in conduct or use language which disrupts, interferes with, is unduly annoying to or prevents the enjoyment or maintenance of State Park Service lands or waters by other visitors. (New Jersey A:s.7:2-2.11)

The 'reasonably prudent person' can also be considered a discursive foil against which immoral conduct can be manufactured. Park agents can evoke and deploy this discursive sensibility to their advantage when dealing with park users, an especially handy tactic in that it removes the burden of proving that the behaviour under question is actually harming anyone. In other words, rangers can act on the belief that behaviour simply has the capacity to offend. Conduct that is constructed as disorderly need only offend the park ranger, who, through the exercise of discretion, can claim the authority to speak for the 'reasonably prudent person' and deem what is offensive. Thus, with the discretion provided to park agents, a regulatory sensibility can be projected anywhere in park space as a personage who represents a standard of reasonableness that, reflexively, has the capacity to be offended. This feature of park ranger authority is embedded in park legislation that allow rangers a wide berth of discretion. For example, in Oregon disorderly noise is defined as the 'operation of any noise-producing machine ... in a manner that in the judgment of the park manager is disturbing to other park visitors' (Oregon A:s. OAR 736-10-045). While the presence of this discursive persona is routinely relied on for the regulation of noises that threaten the 'peace and quiet' of nature,[10] it is perhaps even more vividly evoked in the moral regulation of conduct that is constituted as indecent.

Decency

Indecency is constituted as a form of conduct where the body is revealed in ways that are considered offensive. Prohibitions against indecent conduct rely on a private/public distinction that segregates conduct involving sex and nudity to the cover of a private sphere; and, as I have indicated, the only sites of legal privacy – aside from washrooms and changehouses – are the shelters erected on campsites. To be decent, then, is to be modest, chaste, discrete, and 'reasonably prudent' when it comes to one's own body. Prohibitions against indecency are centred around injunctions forbidding sexual activities in public, and restrictions on nudity and nakedness. Oregon legislation provides a good example of the former:

> A person commits the crime of public indecency if while in, or in view of, a public place the person performs: An act of sexual intercourse ... An act of deviate sexual intercourse ... An act exposing the genitals of the person with the intent of arousing the sexual desire of the person or another person. (Oregon A:s. OAR 736-10-45, s.1(a)(b)(c))[11]

And the State of Florida supplies an example of the latter:

> In every area of a park including bathing areas no individual shall expose the human male or female genitals, pubic area, the entire buttocks or female breasts below the top of the nipple, with less than a fully opaque covering. (Florida A:s.16D-2.004 (2)(e))

The disorder present here is one of displaced conduct, where otherwise acceptable behaviour – having sex and being naked – causes a disorder when displaced from private into public spaces. Ironically, this regulatory concern seems to stem, in part, from the fact that the possibility of people exposing themselves is all the greater when park space is rendered so open and so publicly visible, with so few private sites. Private activities, such as changing, urinating, or having sex could accidentally become public due to the open, visible nature of organized campgrounds and beach areas.[12] A concern with decency is often expressed in sporadic prohibitions against loiterers and peeping Toms who seem to present a threat because their idleness presupposes some sort of morally offensive intent.[13] These efforts to enforce decency are an effect of the strict segregating of day and night conduct, which gives legal privacy to the heterosexual family campsite. There is also a tone of titillation that runs through these regulations, a fear that the very sight of a bare breast or buttocks could excite the viewer into dangerous sexual action.

A curious aberration in the literature occurs in a California statute that regulates indecent conduct. It reads:

> No person shall appear nude ... except in authorized areas set aside for that purpose by the Department. The word nude as used herein means unclothed or in such a state of undress as to expose any part of portion of the *public* [*sic*] *or anal region* or genitalia of any person or any portion of the breast at or below the areola of any female person. (California B: s.4322; emphasis added)

This obvious error, the substitution of 'public' for 'pubic,' while humorous, is also quite instructive in reminding us of the socially constructed nature of what is understood as 'the public.' Thomas Mitchell, in discussing the encoding of violence in public space, reminds us that the ideal of the classic public sphere has always depended upon the exclusion of certain groups, the most conspicuous of these being women and visible minorities. 'The very notion of the "public,"' writes Mitchell, 'grows out of a conflation of two very different words, *populo*, (the people) and *pubes* (adult men). The word *public* might more properly be written with the 'l' in parentheses to remind us that, for much of human history political and social authority has derived from a "pubic" sphere and not a public one. This seems to be the case even when the public sphere is personified as a female figure' (Mitchell 1994b:379).

This conflation is even more striking in terms of 'the public' promoted within the 'natural' environment of parks, a naturalness that is often personified as female, typically in phrases such as 'virgin forests' and 'mother earth.' Discourses that are concerned with vices such as indecency, which rely on a notion of 'the public' are also discourses of domination, where patriarchal 'pubic' power is exercised through a particular conception of 'the public.'

Hygiene and Sanitation

Regulatory efforts concerned with hygiene and sanitation represent some of the most interesting regulatory discourses in the park literature. I utilize an intentionally broad interpretation of what hygiene denotes; I use the term to mean a prescribed routine of behaviour that works towards a state of health and cleanliness. Thus, along with littering offences, I also consider behaviour that defaces, damages, or removes park objects, both natural and human-made, as unhygienic in that such behaviour disorders the aesthetic appearance of park space and deviates from a park hygiene in which compliant visitors are expected to participate.

The offence of littering is the most common prohibition having to do with keeping the park 'clean.' Littering offences are often specific in nature. Two examples:

> No person shall leave, deposit, drop, or scatter bottles, broken glass, ashes, waste paper, cans, or other litter in a unit except in a receptacle designated for that purpose, and no person shall import any litter, or import and deposit any litter into or in any unit from other places. (California B:s. 4310)

> No person shall deposit liquid or solid waste matter in a provincial park or other recreation area except in a receptacle or area provided for that purpose by the Minister. (Alberta C:s.12(1))

The offence of littering involves the depositing of refuse, of material that has been discarded after an act of consumption has taken place. Complementing these general littering prohibitions are more specific injunctions against defacing, damaging, or removing of natural or man-made objects. For example:

> Except with the permission of the Minister, no person while in the park shall ... cut, damage or remove any plant, shrub, flower or

tree ... remove any artifact or object of natural curiosity or interest ... remove, damage or deface any real or personal property
belonging to or claimed by the Crown or other persons. (Nova
Scotia A:s.22(a)(b)(g))

Exceptions are often made for authorized uses of 'park objects'
for educational or commercial use:

Unless specifically authorized by the Department for management,
research or educational purposes, the cutting, injuring, or removal
of trees, shrubs, wildflowers, ferns, mosses, or other plants from
lands administered by the Division is prohibited. Also prohibited is
the defacing, damaging, removing, or altering any structures, buildings, natural land features, or other park property or equipment, or
the willful harming, collecting, or possessing of wildlife, flora or
fauna. (Delaware A:s.15.1(c))

Thus, regulations such as this one make it possible for park
authorities to prosecute a camper for chopping a single branch
off a tree for use as a marshmallow stick, while logging companies
within the same park can legitimately carry out extensive clear-
cutting and selective cutting operations under the pretext of
'resource management.' These regulations seem to make little
distinction between built objects such as signs and buildings, and
natural landscape objects such as plants or rocks – 'man-made'
objects such as park signs are viewed as being as important to the
'natural' landscape of the park as a stand of trees.
    Regulations dealing with sanitation are more specifically con-
cerned with contaminating behaviour, where people may come in
contact with the waste products of others. Two of the most common activities park regulators target are the washing of dirty
dishes and soiled clothes at public water taps and open beaches.
For example:

No person shall clean fish or food, clean or wash dishes, clothing,
or articles at hydrants, fountains, water taps or water faucets located
in restrooms, bathhouses or attached to stand pipes or buildings ...

[This section] also applies to all trailer dump stations, streams and springs. (Massachusetts A:s.12.14 (2))[14]

Prohibitions against cleaning and gutting fish are often explicit:

Cleaning fish at campground hydrants or any other facility not specifically for that purpose is prohibited. All fish entrails or other inedible fish parts shall be disposed of in an appropriate fish cleaning station or trash can. (Utah H:s.R651-624-5)

Thus, these prohibitions are centred around forms of 'dirt' such as food waste, soiled water, and fish entrails, which could easily contaminate the very places – such as water taps and swimming areas – people look to for some sense of cleansing and purity. Beyond this concern with the unsanitary features of washing and cleaning in public are extensive sanitary prohibitions having to do with the depositing of both human and pet excrement. The majority of prohibitions against human defecation indicate that 'body waste' or 'excrement' must be deposited in 'the receptacles provided for the purpose' (Alabama A:220-5-.06). For example:

Depositing, except into receptacles provided for that purpose, any body waste, or depositing any bottles, cans, clothes, rags, metal, wood, stone, or other damaging substance in any fixture in any restroom or other structure is prohibited. (South Carolina A:s.1 (f)(5))

Often these prohibitions are qualified – a lower standard of sanitation is tolerated – when referring to 'less civilized' areas of the park. For example, 'Urinating or defecating other than at the places provided is prohibited,' states a Tennessee (A) regulation, 'except in backcountry wilderness or other remote areas.' Indeed, as I discuss in Chapter 3, 'primitive,' 'wild,' and 'undeveloped' areas of the park are often defined in terms of a lack of 'civilized' toilet facilities. What is interesting about these qualifiers is that they assert that the campground is not as wild as the rest of the park, an admission that is notably absent in other injunctions.

The scatological confusion addressed in these regulations mirrors the general contradiction of park space: portrayed and presented as 'wilderness,' park landscape is in fact a highly constructed, hygienic landscape where everything within the space is ordered.

The primary rationalization behind pet regulation is that domesticated animals of course cannot be counted on to defecate in designated places, and they present a constant threat of contamination, especially in areas where people, and especially children, eat, swim, and play.[15] Widespread prescriptions require park users to restrain their animals with leashes, or within cages and crates, to keep pets out of areas such as beaches, picnic grounds and playgrounds, and to require that pet owners 'clean up' after their pets.[16] For example, in Wisconsin:

> No person may allow a dog, cat or other pet in any building or any bathing beach, picnic area, playground ... Dogs, cats and other pets shall be kept on a leash not more then 8 feet long and under control at all times in all other state park areas, headquarters areas, ranger stations, campgrounds, on posted trails ... Persons bringing or allowing pets in designated use areas shall be responsible for proper removal and disposal in sanitary facilities of any waste produced by these animals. (Wisconsin A:s.NR45.06)[17]

Additionally, pet owners are prohibited from allowing their pets to 'interfere in any manner with the enjoyment of the area by others' (Wisconsin, A:NR45.06), including having pets that are noisy, intimidating, or vicious. Park authorities are given widespread power to seize, remove, destroy, and dispose of domestic pets that contravene these provisions.

Beyond this concern with sanitation, the regulation of pets works to re-enforce the difference between domesticated, captive animals which people bring into the park as pets, and the free, 'natural' animals that exist as part of the 'wild,' naturally dangerous environment of the park. Yet, at the same time this distinction is often blurred by the tamed, pet-like qualities of park wildlife that have become sensitized to visitors. This confusion is nicely illustrated by the frequent prohibitions such as 'Do Not Feed the

Wildlife,' which contrast with the providing of food and water to domesticated pets.[18] Indeed, the sign that reads 'Do Not Feed The Bears' has come to stand as a kind of sad emblem indicating that even the most 'dangerous' and wild of park creatures have often become sensitized to and dependent on gawking, crust-throwing tourists. The demeaning of wild creatures in the name of human entertainment is vividly evoked in Canadian poet Alden Nowlans's poem 'The Bull Moose,' in which he describes the treatment of a dying bull moose at the hands of townspeople just before wardens arrive:

> The young men snickered and tried to pour beer
> down his throat, while their girl friends
> took their pictures ...
> When the wardens came, everyone agreed it was a shame
> to shoot anything so shaggy and cuddlesome.
> He looked like the kind of pet
> women put to bed with their sons. (1982:129)

Park legislation often attempts to re-enforce the difference between domestic animals that have human owners, and the 'free' *wild*life of the park. For example, in Georgia, '"Pet" means those taxa [*sic*] of animals which have traditionally lived in a state of dependence on and under the domination and control of humans and have been kept as tame pets, including cats and dogs. The term pet does not include animals raised as livestock. Animals which live in a captive or tame state and which lack a genetic distinction from members of the same taxon living in the wild are presumptively wild animals' (Georgia D:s.391-5-2.02 (p)). Other notable examples include the definition of 'domestic animal' as 'an animal that is kept under human control or by habit or training lives in association with man'; 'wildlife' as 'a species of vertebrate which is wild by nature and hence not normally dependent on man directly to provide its food, shelter and water' (Nova Scotia (B:s.3(g)(o)); also 'animal' meaning a 'domestic animal, [one] that is wild by nature but has been domesticated' (Alberta C:s.1(c)). The occasional pet or animal definition borders on the bizarre. For example, in California, 'An animal is any animate being which is endowed with the power of voluntary motion; animate being, not human' (California B:s.4301 (p)). The effort to regulate domestic pets constructs an image of wild animals as living in the park independent of human influence, in a state of wildness and freedom, an image that posits the park landscape as a permanent 'wildness' which remains unaffected by the transient recreation of park users.

The presence of pets in a park setting not only reveals the tamed, pet-like nature of park animals that have been sensitized to human conduct – a contradiction that pet regulations attempt to address by re-enforcing the distinction between the domestic and wild – but is also seen to be a threat to the 'wild' animals, as illustrated by the widespread prohibitions against domesticated animals who 'chase and molest' wild animals. Strangely, domestic animals must be restrained in order to protect the undomesticated, wild animals of the park. So while the danger of 'wild' animals is often evoked as part of the 'natural' and 'dangerous' park environment, it is the presence and subsequent regulation of domestic animals that more sharply dramatizes a wild and untamed park environment.

More subtly, the regulation of domesticated animals acts as a discursive referent for acceptable human conduct, constructing disorderly human behaviour as animal-like. This is especially striking considering that the prohibitions concerning human and pet defecation read almost exactly the same, except that pets must rely on their human masters to deposit their feces into the proper receptacles.

Alcohol and Fire

The regulatory themes of quietness, decency, and hygiene are vividly expressed in two popular campaigns of park order which target the use of fire and the consumption of alcohol. In both cases, neither fire nor alcohol can be directly moralized as 'evil' or 'destructive' in itself. Rather, the conduct of individuals consuming alcohol or using fire is moralized in terms of the three main themes of park governance. The presence of fire and alcohol allows park regulators to carry out extensive campaigns that constantly evoke both personal and environmental risk and promote the need for self-regulation and control.

Alcohol has a long and distinguished career in the history of moral regulation, from the early temperance movement discussed by Gusfield (1963) to the advent of the anti–drunk driver movement exemplified by the rise of Mothers Against Drunk Driving (MADD).[19] Certainly, the persona of the evil drunk driver has provided moral entrepreneurs with a sustainable character to animate discourses of regulation, from school officials and the police who construct a reckless image of the teenage driver, to distillery associations who promote 'safe drinking' as part of their marketing campaigns demonstrating responsible corporate citizenship. The drunk driver has become a favourite target of moral entrepreneurs in the public sphere, a key figure in the dramatization of moralizing discourses that act to 'responsibilize' individual behaviour.[20]

The restriction and prohibition of alcohol within parks is an exemplar of the accumulative effect of the moral discourses that order conduct. To promote sobriety through the restriction of alcohol consumption is to order 'noise,' enforce decency, and promote hygiene. The discursive personage of the 'reasonable decent person,' is undoubtedly a sober one. To evoke the immorality of alcohol 'abuse' is to link a whole juggernaut of moral tropes that can be deployed in powerful ensembles of moral regulation.

Park legislation explicitly links alcohol consumption to the spectre of disorderly conduct; these links often specifically emphasize the moral quality of decency.[21] A state of Florida regulation provides a typical example:

> Persons in any park who are intoxicated or who conduct themselves in a destructive, disorderly, offensive, obscene, or profane manner are considered public nuisances and are subject to arrest and/or ejection from the park. Common moral decency is the criterion for determining such public nuisance. (Florida: As.-16D-2.007(2))

It is important to stress the degree of moral panic associated with alcohol use in parks. Park administrators consistently named 'alcohol abuse,' alcohol 'indulgence,' and the 'alcohol problem' as the major issue in keeping order in parks.[22] A Canadian park co-ordinator's viewpoint epitomizes the perception of an alcohol problem: 'We here at the St Lawrence Parks Commission are dedicated to providing quiet, family oriented campsites that allow people to enjoy a relaxing vacation without interruptions ... Continued problems with youth "parties" have been experienced in certain parks for many years. With the assistance of local OPP detachments, we have instituted a "zero" tolerance enforcement for our alcohol ban and regular revision of the alcohol ban to reduce much of the rowdyism and vandalism in our parks' (Parks of the St Lawrence C). The fact that authorities can *revise a ban* speaks to the expansive nature of the regulatory practice of banning: once a particular object is banned (alcohol), one can also ban various forms of conduct associated with an object (transporting alcohol). Thus, while seeming absolute, the ban can be used to include an ever-expanding spectrum of conduct associated with the initial object of prohibition.

The use of alcohol is often linked to the problems of youth parties and under-age drinking, and is seen to accompany offences such as vandalism and rowdyism.[23] Park managers stress how parks which are located closer to large cities tend to have 'urban type' problems which often involve alcohol.[24] Surprisingly few administrators mentioned the problem of drinking and driving; those that did mention it in reference to initiatives undertaken in cooperation with an outside police agency.[25]

The strategies utilized to regulate alcohol usage range from the permitting of alcohol consumption only in specific places, usually the 'residence' of the campsite, to the banning of alcohol consumption at certain times or in certain places, either on a permanent basis, as illustrated in Figure 9, or in the form of temporary bans that take place during traditional party weekends, such as 24 May. Often alcohol is banned from campgrounds that are designated for families. Liquor prohibitions construct young adults, especially males and college students, as the prime offenders against 'family camping,' as depicted in Figure 9. A group of guys standing around drinking beer comes to represent disorderly behaviour. It would not likely take much *visual noise* for their presence to be deemed a disorder that should be removed from the park. Hard liquor is often prohibited, as is the use of beer kegs, which would encourage a party atmosphere.

The regulatory effort against alcohol consumption, which in some cases manifests a temperance mentality, is complemented by prohibitions against the presence of intoxicated bodies in the park. For example, in Washington State, '[b]eing, or remaining in, or loitering about in any state park area while in a state of intoxication shall be prohibited' (B:s.WAC 352-32-230); and in South Carolina, 'Unlawful acts in state parks' include 'Entering or remaining within the limits of the park facility while in an intoxicated or drugged condition' (A:s.1(L)). These injunctions are quite remarkable in that they enforce sobriety as the ideal state of consciousness needed to experience the 'natural' environment of the park. Additionally, by targeting the bodies of park users, and not just the act of alcohol consumption itself, authorities are able to exert extra control over private consumption: you might be able to drink behind your tent flaps, but after you emerge your liquored-up body will be illegal.

More implicitly, these injunctions work to connect and enforce a homology between the polluting of the body with alcohol and the polluting of the natural environment of the park with disorderly conduct that threatens what is 'natural.' The moral regulation of alcohol relies on the image of 'the drunk' whose bodily boundaries blur and break down in a disorderly scene of audible and visual noise, lewdness, and sexual danger, all of which wreck the hygiene of the ordered park space. In contrast, the sober park user is quiet, decent, and clean, a compliant body existing without question within the order of designated space, the individual's personal conduct 'responsibilized' within a context of environmental consciousness. Alcohol regulation is carried out by the simultaneous policing of both the boundaries of park space and the human body in a way which polices 'common moral decency.'

A strikingly ironic feature of the construction of the 'alcohol problem' in parks is how the legitimacy and expansion of regulatory efforts seem to depend on regulatory failure. A major goal of park government is to secure further regulatory efforts by demonstrating how the present effort can fail or how unsuccessful it has been, a trend illustrated repeatedly in park documents.

'The use of alcohol is the major source of most of our enforcement problems. Several of our parks have alcohol bans,' states an Indiana park director, 'and we will be looking more toward these types of preventive measures in the months and years to come' (Indiana: B).[26] In arguing for the 'technique' of inspecting car trunks for alcohol at the park gate for the 24 May weekend, an Ontario park manager stated: 'Observations of last year's Victoria Day weekend from a few park superintendents suggest a problem in some parks persists with allowing vehicles to enter when there is a high suspicion alcohol may be present. We know that officers do not have the authority to open and search the trunk ... It's intended that officers will not be conducting a search of the vehicles, but visitors will voluntarily agree to show the officer the contents of trunks and coolers' (Ontario E). Thus, the failure to enact a total prohibition on the possession of alcohol is used as justification for more extensive and intrusive techniques which then re-enforce an attitude of 'high suspicion' among enforcement staff. Accompanying this proposal was a diagram of proposed official graffiti to be posted at the front gate warning of 'vehicle search,' along with a 'Script for Interviewing Visitors at Park Entrance Victoria Day Weekend' (Ontario D), which reads, in part:

> HI! Welcome to _____ Provincial Park ... You know ... that one of the conditions for camping this weekend is that Alcohol is prohibited in the park ... Do you have any Alcohol in this vehicle?'

> If yes – I'm sorry I cannot allow you to enter the park until you dispose of the Alcohol (provide instructions/options).

> If no – WILL YOU SHOW ME THAT YOU DON'T HAVE ANY ALCOHOL IN THE TRUNK?

NOTICE

Alcoholic Beverage Ban

Campgrounds in the   —   State Park system are established and operated to provide registered campers with a natural setting where they may enjoy rest, relaxation, and recreation.

The Parks Division of the   —   Department of Natural Resources is deeply concerned that many campers cannot enjoy their camping experience because of the indiscriminate use of alcoholic beverages by some park visitors.

So that a better atmosphere for camping may be established, the Director of the Department of Natural Resources has issued a legal order prohibiting alcoholic beverages in all portions of this park.

We realize this will inconvenience some park users, but it is the intent of this ban to return to the park the peace and tranquility necessary for a quality recreational experience.

We ask for your cooperation in helping to enforce this order and are quite certain that your stay will be more pleasant and enjoyable.

Parks Division
Department of Natural Resources

6/19/73

Figure 9 Alcohol Beverage Ban notice

Possible Response: No! or, You can't search my vehicle.

[Rejoinder]: I'M NOT ASKING TO SEARCH YOUR VEHICLE I'm asking you to show me that you don't have any Alcohol in your trunk (or in the back of the vehicle, e.g., van, trunk).

And what if I don't?

[Rejoinder]: YOU WON'T BE ABLE TO ENTER THE PARK.

This technique vividly illustrates the promotion of self-regulation and self-inspection by park authorities, where individuals are 'expected to inspect' their own conduct. Additionally, this technique evokes a general 'reverse onus' climate, where individuals must constantly exhibit their allegiance to the mission of parks by conducting themselves in the prescribed way. The zealousness that results from an enforcement environment of 'high suspicion' can take on comic forms. In searching out illegal alcohol consumption one Massachusetts ranger recommends hourly foot patrols because he has found that to avoid detection 'creative violators have been known to use, but [have not been] limited to, the following deceptions: Coca Cola wrappers, plain cups, picnic jugs, trash barrels, spare tires, and baby carriages' (Massachusetts A:29).

Remarkably, in Canada during the Victoria Day weekend, this scheme was approved for use by government lawyers who relied on a Supreme Court ruling that upheld the validity of similar 'volunteer' searches during a rock concert at Maple Leaf Gardens in Toronto.[27] The irony of such a search would surely not be lost on park visitors who arrive at park gates with expectations of escaping surveillance typical of city entertainment.

The regulation of fire is another fascinating aspect of park governance, as it targets a threatening symbol of transgression. Alcohol threatens to blur only the boundaries of the body, causing a chorus of disorderly conduct; fire is capable of consuming boundaries and destroying the designated quality of park space. The use of fire for cooking and warmth in parks is a major feature of the experience of camping; to burn wood in the open air and watch the flames and smoke, to smell food cooking on fire, is to partake of an activity that is reserved for places where nature is to be experienced. Park fire is constituted as a wild, natural force that is to be ignited, tamed and controlled by park users; it is in contrast to fire in urban spaces which is harnessed within internal combustion engines and gas ranges. Indeed, outdoor fires within the city usually evoke images of the homeless and transient as well occurences of protest and civil disorder.[28] Use of the metaphor 'the city is burning' to describe inner city rioting has a deep resonance in the public psyche.

Certainly, the risk evoked by the use of fire in parks draws implicitly on the danger fire appears to pose in urban settings, where it is often seen as evil and unnatural. For example, when occupants of a house die in an urban fire one often feels the fire itself is to blame. To govern how people use fire is to confirm that 'natural forces' are dangerous and capable of great havoc and damage.

The regulation of fire in parks provides an example of an activity that is very tightly tied to the principal designated site of control: the fire*place*. Three prescriptions are widespread concerning the use of fire by park visitors: that fires may only be lit and burned within designated places, that fires must be attended by a competent individual, and that fires must be extinguished when they are to be left unused. A typical statute states:

> The lighting or maintaining of a fire is prohibited except: In designated camping and picnicking areas when the fire is confined in a fireplace or grill provided for that purpose ... All fires shall be completely extinguished when not in use. Leaving a fire unattended is prohibited. (Utah H:s.R651-613-1; s.R651-613-2)

Additionally, there are widespread prohibitions against the littering of fire, 'throwing or discarding lighted or smouldering material' (Oklahoma, A: s.725:30-4-7), or 'dropping a lighted cigarette' (Tennessee A: s.0400-2-2-.12). While these prohibitions only occasionally mention smoking, it is clear that the littering of pipe ash and smouldering cigarettes is the main target.[29] Fire also provides an opportunity for park authorities to practise the technique of banning: under certain circumstances they can simply prohibit the presence of fire, and revoke the rule allowing open fires at designated fireplaces.

Quite often, legislation does not just order that fire not be left unattended, but that it be attended by a person who is 'competent,' or 'over the age of 16.'[30] This prescribing of competency evokes the theme of carelessness that is widespread in forest fire prevention efforts. The trope of carelessness is frequently evoked in official graffiti posted along public highways, which portrays the consequences of carelessness. For example, the Ontario signage in Figure 10 portrays a burnt out, wasted landscape (Hermer and Hunt 1996).

However, the theme of carelessness is most vividly brought to mind by one of the most distinct figures of moral regulation in North America, Smokey Bear. A brief history of Smokey, and the rules that govern the use of his costume in North American parks, vividly illustrate the ways in which fire regulation calls forth a nexus of personal and environmental risks. According to Stephen Pyne (1982: 176–7), in July 1942, United States Secretary of Agriculture Claude R.R. Rickard announced in a radio broadcast that 'the control and prevention of forest fires is a first line defense job on the home front ... We cannot forget ... that the British Royal Air Force found it worthwhile to start great fires in the forests of Germany. Every fire in our fields or forests this year is an enemy fire.' While the connection between forest fire prevention and national defence had for some time become synonymous in the public mindset with slogans such as 'Careless Matches Aid the Axis' and 'Your Match, Their Secret Weapon,' this moral campaign lacked its own unique symbol (176). In 1944 the Wartime Ad Council and the Co-Operative Forest Fire Prevention Campaign, with the help of an advertising consultant, came up with the idea of using a bear after considering other animals, including squirrels and monkeys. The artist contracted to create Smokey was instructed by forest service and war council bureaucrats that this bear should wear 'a campaign hat' and have 'an appealing expression' with 'a knowledgeable but quizzical look,' and should not

Figure 10 'Carelessness Costs' sign (Photo by author)

look like 'the bear that symbolized Russia.' The first poster of the uniformed bear, named after a famous New York City fireman, 'Smokey Joe' Martin, was issued in 1945 (176). However, it was 1950 when a real bear became the ultimate referent for the poster. An abandoned bear cub, saved from a forest fire by a ranger, became 'Little Smokey,' and upon delivery to Washington National Zoo, soon became a legend. At the height of his popularity, in the mid-1960s, a poll indicated that Smokey was the most recognizable figure in America, and the Smokey Bear Act was passed by Congress to protect America's beloved icon from 'commercial exploitation' (177). Despite efforts to provide the famous bear with a mate – her name was Goldie – Smokey left no offspring and died in captivity in 1977. By then Smokey had become one of the most popular exports of American consumer culture, and his persona was exported, to Canada, Mexico, and Turkey. Smokey was even introduced by missionaries to the people of the Belgian Congo, where children were reported to be 'intensely interested in the bear that wore a hat, and wondered if all animals in America wore hats' (179–80).

Every summer, Smokey Bear costumes are dispatched in crates to parks across North America to be animated in 'visitor service' and 'nature interpretation' programs. Accompanying 'Smokey' is a most notable governance text, *Guidelines for the Use of the Smokey Costume* (Ontario E), a list of rules park staff are expected to follow when suited up in the Smokey costume. These rules nicely illustrate the important distinctions, made by H.L.A. Hart (1961), between primary and secondary rules – those that order regulatory objects, and those that regulate the agents of regulation.

The secondary 'Smokey rules' have three main prescriptive goals: (1) to regulate the character of the person wearing the costume; (2) to order the performance that Smokey carries out, and (3) to prescribe the role of all assistants taking part in each performance. The wearer of the Smokey costume, who should 'be tall' (Ontario E: 1994:2) is expected to behave in a manner that does not soil Smokey's image. The wearer is warned, apparently without irony, that the rules allow 'no alcohol or cigarettes during

Smokey performances,' and that Smokey 'Be alive, [v]igorous, [and] alert.' The rules go on to say: 'remember, you are presenting one of the greatest of all symbols. You are a celebrity, a star. Act like one; don't destroy the image' (3). Smokey must always be in full constume, as well – no half dressed bears are allowed – and wearers are warned not to 'appear before your cue,' a perfect reminder of the dramaturgical nature of Smokey's presentation. Wearers are also told: 'Know the route you are going to take so that Smokey looks alert, not lost,' and move him about 'carefully so as not to upset the children.' Do not 'stand with your hands at your side,' but rather 'hold them up and move them about. Wave to people.' In a tone that suggests the wearer might somehow be losing his human sense, the rule writer also suggests that 'A handshake is a useful device for activity' (Ontario E: 1994:3).

With the character of the wearer secure, and his movements prescribed, the role of an assistant is emphasized. Smokey should always be accompanied by an assistant, one that will 'let Smokey lead' and 'keep crowds from him ... they tend to maul his suit.' (In a regulated wilderness it is the friendly bear who is in danger of being mauled.) Most importantly, 'an assistant should do all the talking. It is best to keep Smokey silent. This helps prevent him from saying anything "dumb," and preserves his image as a bear. Bears don't talk' (Ontario E: 1994:2).

This anthropomorphic performance constructs Smokey with an unassailable moral character, made even more admirable because he is also a civilized bear. He is indeed the perfect authority to communicate the risks of both human and non-human worlds: he is rendered inhuman by his inability to speak, and tame by his adoption of the niceties of human interaction. Smokey is the epitome of moderation; he is punctual, polite, nicely groomed, good with children – a picture of self-control and personal responsibility. Think what his opposite would be: a rude, slothful, badly dressed bear, drinking and smoking, stumbling, lost without human assistance, frightening children with his attempts at human speech.

Smokey's character, which is used to invoke the dangers of carelessness, promotes a central characteristic of park order: the promotion of self-regulation. The promotion of self-governance is vividly illustrated in Smokey's slogan, which dates back to 1947: 'Remember, ONLY YOU can prevent forest fires.' The slogan was often accompanied by a picture of Smokey standing against a shovel, pointing, like Uncle Sam, at the reader. It is strikingly similar to another warning central to the regulation of leisure: 'ONLY YOU can stop drinking and driving.' And, like discourses of alcohol regulation, fire itself the object through which conduct is ordered. In other words, Smokey Bear is not so much concerned with actually regulating fire as he is with ordering behaviour, just as impaired-driving crusaders focus on the dubious character of the drunk driver.

This environment of self-regulation, communicated through the stoic character of Smokey, promotes a climate of surveillance where individuals are encouraged to self-police themselves as well as the 'strangers' around them. This risk-based surveillance is most vividly expressed in the presence of neighbourhood watch – style programs which are popular in many parks. Often, 'park watch' programs utilize their own animal mascots, some of whom look like they could have been rejects from the original Smokey campaign; for example, Maryland state parks utilize McGruff the Crime Dog to encourage visitors to participate in 'park watch,' and to 'take a more active role in protecting personal property and preserving the park' (see Figure 11). The dual emphasis here, which invokes both environmental preservation and personal protection, is especially notable in park jurisdictions. The binding together of personal and environmental risk, where one works both to secure the self and to save the environment, provides for a powerful moral emphasis. As a civilized 'celebrity' of the 'wilderness' designed to greet the park visitor (see Figure 12), Smokey Bear stands as a disturbing image, one that depicts only the degraded, emasculated, 'dancing bear' of emparked nature.[31]

The Risk of Nature

As we have seen, within the designated space of park jurisdictions, the conduct of park visitors is subject to regulatory efforts that

Numerous towns and cities across the nation have instituted a program called **CRIME WATCH**. The idea behind this program is to encourage residents to keep an eye on their neighbors' property and to report any suspicious activities to the local or state police. Everyone makes a commitment to look out for the welfare of others.

The State Forest and Park Service has implemented a similar program called **PARK WATCH**. The objective of **PARK WATCH** is to encourage park visitors and neighbors to take a more active role in protecting personal property and preserving the park. You are being asked to be more alert to suspicious activities, vandalism and safety hazards. If you observe ant of these in the park, we ask you to let us know. Report what you see to any park employee or call one of the phone numbers listed below.

The emergency phone numbers for your park are:
Park Ranger ~ 1-800-825-PARK

McGruff Says
"Together we can keep your Maryland State Forests and Parks a safe and enjoyable place for all."

You Can Help:
❏ Display this brochure in your car or camper window as a warning to would-be criminals

❏ Be alert to suspicious activities, vandalism or safety hazards

❏ Don't tempt thieves; store valuables such as cameras, radios, purses, etc., out of sight

❏ Don't take Action yourself. If you observe someone breaking park rules contact a Park Ranger

❏ Report incidents as soon as possible

McGruff, The Crime Dog

Figure 11   McGruff the Crime Dog brochure (Courtesy of the Maryland Department of Natural Resources)

Figure 12 Smokey Bear signage instructions (Courtesy of the Minnesota Department of Natural Resources)

promote the qualities of quietness, decency, and hygiene. The promotion of these three themes intersect in such a way that the ordering of conduct is consistently linked to the construction of the park as 'natural.' Through the intense regulation of visitor conduct, the 'natural' environment of the park is dramatized. To be quiet, to refrain from making any sort of audible or visual noise promotes the 'natural' qualities of quiet and peacefulness. To be clean and sanitary promotes the park as a pure, hygienic place which has been 'discovered' and cannot be disturbed or polluted. To act 'decently' promotes the park as a moral space which is sacred, and thus at risk of defilement.

A key aspect of the dramatization of 'the natural' through the ordering of conduct is the constant promotion of self-regulation in an environment where both personal and environmental risk are bound together. What is so notable about the socially constructed risks of parks is their reflexive nature. Visitors are not just at risk from the 'wild,' 'natural' environment of the park, but they are also at risk from those who are present within this wilderness, including themselves.

At the same time, the 'natural' environment of the park is always at risk from the conduct of visitors. Wilderness is constructed within this circuit of self-perpetrating risk which relies on regulatory discourses that evoke hazards to both personal and environmental health. The result is the construction of an environmental consciousness that is highly ascetic, where every personal act is connected to the fate of the environment. This asceticism is vividly illustrated in Figure 13, which depicts a landscape that has fallen into a state of anarchy, where disorderly conduct threatens the peace and quiet of a pure nature. 'This is what could happen,' warns the brochure ominously, 'if the public use regulations are not followed.'

What is remarkable about this illustration is the implication that if only park visitors could exercise a minimal degree of recreational self-control in their 'relationship' with nature, the environment would remain in a preserved state. The possibility that the natural world is threatened by systematic pollution from outside the park is not even present. This promotion of self-

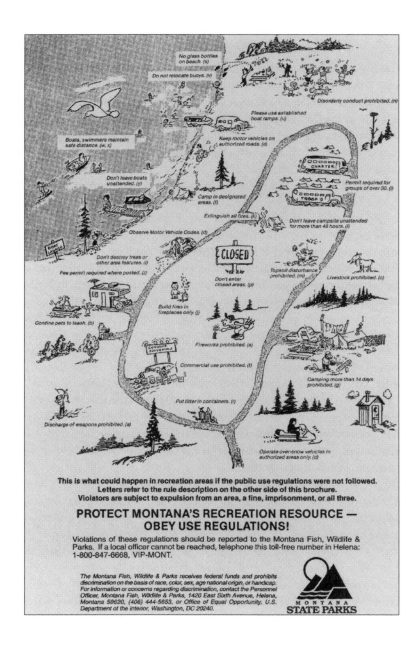

Figure 13 A Guide to Montana's Public Use Regulations (Courtesy of Montana Department of Fish, Wildlife, and Parks)

regulation is intimately tied to the idea that wilderness is a natural system that in itself is self-regulating. This is best illustrated in a Yukon handout that warns of the risks that await hikers: 'Be especially wary of what may seem to be orphaned young. In all likelihood the mother is nearby. Any attempts to "help" could elicit a protective attack from the mother – whether owl, moose or grizzly! Under all circumstances, *it's best to let the laws of the wilderness take their course*' (Yukon A; emphasis added). These 'laws of the wilderness' underlie the idea that wilderness is self-regulating, that wilderness is governed by its own laws that are beyond human governance and control, that it is a site of 'natural law' that cannot be substantially altered by the efforts of humans.

The presence of 'natural laws' is present in both 'corrupt' and 'pure' metaphors of wilderness. Civil authorities often talk about the wilderness of inner cities being beyond the control of police forces and service agencies. Scientists refer to certain forms of bewildering mental illness – where patients wander in their own wilderness – as beyond the reach of modern pharmaceutical technologies. Park mangers warn campers of the precautions that should be taken before being subject to the 'laws of mother nature' when they enter a park. A peculiar homology exists between discourses of self-regulation promoted by park government, epitomized by 'stay on the path' signs, and the promotion of wilderness as being governed by its own laws, which are outside the domain of human action.

The connotation is that self-regulation is a natural state to which people must adhere if they are to protect park nature. This homology generates the effect that the self-regulating conduct of the park user is 'natural' and 'normal' because this self-regulation is mirrored in the natural image of a 'self-governing' wilderness, which, like the 'natural' behaviour of 'man,' has its own 'laws.' Thus, parks can be thought of not just as preserves of what is socially constructed as nature, but also as what is often socially constructed as a 'natural' or 'normal' state of society. This not only includes the so-called 'normal' things such as the traditional family, the suburb, the sober body, but also, more importantly, the idea that it is normal for natural landscapes to be exploited in a regulated manner. Perhaps even more ironic is the connotation that in the very places where we expect to experience freedom it is normal that we should be subject to intense and intrusive forms of regulation. The regulation of park conduct constructs both nature as an object of regulated exploitation, and the accompanying idea of freedom as a state achieved through compliance to authority.

CHAPTER FIVE

The Emparkment of Order

Wilderness, in the final analysis, is a state of mind.
Roderick Nash, *Wilderness and the American Mind*

Thanks for helping keep the 'WILD' in wilderness.
Yukon Wilderness Travellers 'No Trace Checklist'

Over the last century, parks have embodied a set of moral values that are viewed, often with great nostalgia, as representing the most enlightened impulses that we are capable of as a society. The idea of collectively protecting spaces, setting them aside in law for our own betterment and for the protection of 'nature,' is often viewed as something that we have 'gotten right' in a society routinely characterized as uncaring and self-interested. Ironically, parks make us feel human at times when our humanity often seems to be in question. That we have managed to get parks so wrong, that parks now act as extraordinary sites for regulatory forms that are complicit with widespread environmental destruction, is emblematic of the paradoxical character of the liberal mode of governance that has emerged at the end of this century.

Throughout this book, I have attempted to examine the geography of emparked nature while staying close to the everyday features and conduct of park experience. In this concluding chapter, I go on to emphasize how emparked nature is congruent with the mentalities that create environmental toxification and then act to provide an alibi for the continuing degradation of the ecological sphere. I argue that we must rethink the irresistible idea that we have a 'relationship' with nature through emparkment projects, a construction that needs to be made visible if we are to seriously comprehend the character and consequences of how nature is experienced at the beginning of the twenty-first century.

A Dangerous Utopia

Emparkment order manufactures nature as an object of regulated exploitation, as a landscape that can be simultaneously protected and consumed in such a way that the preservation of nature depends upon its exploitation: an image of nature epitomized by the emblem of 'the rule tree.' This representation depends upon a multitude of invested forms that empark landscape as an image of 'the natural' in order to create a homogeneous, sanitized landscape. Certainly the immutable mobiles used by park governance (laws, policies, standing orders, maps) represent an army of absent experts (foresters, cartographers, tourism advocates, legislators) who work to empark a conception of 'nature' that can be constituted and exploited through regulatory practices. The mythical figure of the forest ranger who sits in his fire tower watching over the forest has been replaced by an array of surveillance technology. Natural resources scientists, utilizing water, air and ore samples, geographic imaging systems, aerial photographs, and terrestrial and aquatic surveys, are able to 'look over' millions of acres without ever setting foot in the forest or on the surface of the lake. Natural features are configured as 'resources' that can be homogenized, quantified, and configured as 'managed' objects.

The mentality of resource management relies heavily on the legitimizing notions of 'sustained yield' and 'carrying capacity,' both of which rely in turn on the idea that nature is a sort of 'zero sum' bank account where interest can be drawn on as long as the principle is not touched. The emparkment of nature through the establishment of public parks relies on an 'optics of regulation,' or the ability of officials to forge and deploy representational technology. As I have demonstrated, emparkment technologies such as official graffiti do not just physically mark space and provide prima facie notice of particular regulations constructed at a distance, but also act to make 'absent things present' by evoking images of wild animals, pathless forests, or other natural spectacles. It is a network of permissions, restrictions, and prohibitions that evoke ever-present risk.

What is most remarkable about how constructed risks represent nature in parks is how regulatory discourses become even more powerful in their ability to 'make up' and evoke wilderness when 'the natural' is perceived as being at risk and in need of protection. The very fear of environmental destruction and personal insecurity further act to arm the discourses of risk with even greater power to represent nature. In the regulated wilderness, risks are constantly described, displayed, promoted, and emphasized. This riskiness, which constructs the 'natural' experience of parks, animates the moral qualities of park regulation that focus on conducting individual visitors as compliant 'customer-violators' who will follow a hygiene of cleanliness, quietness, and decency, themes that construct a 'natural' landscape.

The emparkment of nature as 'regulated wilderness' is truly an expression of what Timothy Mitchell (1991:xii) has referred to as the 'peculiar metaphysics of modernity.' Mitchell's description of the British colonization of Egypt as the 'world as exhibition' brilliantly captures how technologies of representation create an 'experience of the real.' Drawing on the work of Heidegger (1977), Mitchell points out that a key aspect of the exhibition is the ordering tactic of 'enframing,' a method of dividing up and containing, or creating, a 'neutral surface or volume called 'space,' a space that is apparently abstract and neutral, a series of inert frames and containers' (44–5). Although Mitchell links enframing with the construction of military barracks and rebuilt villages, enframing can be considered a basic feature of projects of emparkment, where 'physical space – even respirable air – has become a surface and volume that can be divided up and marked out into places where individuals are positioned' (78). The world as exhibition relies on the discernability between 'the original and the real,' where exhibitional practices establish 'the certainty of representation itself' (171).

The representational power exercised by park government is vividly demonstrated in the exhibitional qualities of governed park space. As official sites where nature is 'preserved,' discourses of park regulation re-enforce the ontological distinction of the exhibition, in the same way that 'regulated wilderness' is represented and dramatized as a 'preserved' specimen of a larger, 'real' wilderness that exists somewhere *outside* of the park.

As the primary ordering tactic in the actualization of park missions, the practice of designating produces an 'exhibition' of wilderness through the effect of enframing. For Mitchell (1991), enframing tends 'to produce the effect of a structure, which seemed to stand apart as something conceptual and prior.' The exhibitional qualities of emparked nature are most commonly demonstrated in the popular behaviour of tourists who take pictures of the 'wild' park landscape: re-framing the enframed. Lookout points and other constructed spectacles – which are often marked with the official graffiti of a camera – attest to the photogenic character of emparked nature. We are reminded of the exhibitional qualities of park landscape by an advertisement in a provincial park brochure (see Figure 14) for disposable 'fun saver' cameras, available at the Nature Nook Book Store, which will capture 'great memories of the outdoors' and 'breathtaking landscapes.' The smiling forest animals in this ad are emblematic of the exploitation of park resources and wild creatures for the benefit of human recreation and entertainment. While Mitchell applied the concept of enframing to the colonization of nineteenth-century Egypt, Heidegger, from whom he adopted the notion, described it in a way that I think even more accurately describes the emparked nature of parks. Heidegger conceptualized enframing as a form of 'revealing,' where people and objects are reduced to a 'standing reserve' that serves modern technology. In his discussion of 'enframing,' Heidegger (1977: 299) provides an example of a forester who could easily be an official of emparked nature: 'the forester who measures the felled timber in the woods and who to all appearances walks the forest path in the same way his grandfather did is today ordered by industry that produces commercial woods, whether he knows it or not. He is

Figure 14 'All Packed ... and Ready to Go' (Courtesy of the Ontario Ministry of Natural Resources)

made subordinate to the orderability of cellulose ... which is then delivered to newspapers and magazines ... so that a set configuration of opinion becomes available on demand.'

Enframing acts to create a population of park users that are subordinated to the needs of consumer culture, to the casting of nature as a commodified object where nature is enjoyed and consumed as an object of entertainment, recreation, and excitement. Emparked nature is subordinated to this 'orderability of cellulose,' to a 'set configuration of opinion' which supports the commodification of natural landscapes. Park nature is an exemplar of what Lefebvre (1991:56) called a 'hygienic ghetto,' where space is 'shown as display, even when it is laid out in lawns and planted with trees.' This 'zero point' of space, and other zero forms such as time and speech, create a 'kind of intellectual and social asceticism' of a frozen landscape that becomes 'abstract space' that is defined not just by 'the disappearance of trees, or by the receding of nature' (50), but by a space of power exercised for the benefit of capital and neo-capitalist enterprises and the 'world of commodities' (53).

As a form of representation, the emparked nature of parks carries out a double role described as 'something like ideology' by Thomas Mitchell. Nature is represented as 'an artificial world as if it were simply given and inevitable.' The artificial, constructed landscape of parks ghettoizes 'nature' as always having been an object of consumer exploitation, an enframed exhibition that objectifies nature. Additionally, parks are landscaped in such a way that people are 'figured' as consumers who are constantly at risk of conducting themselves as polluters in a 'pathless' landscape. The sanitized, homogenized landscape of parks, where both space and behaviour are conducted as decent, clean, and quiet, has the effect of constituting the wildness of wilderness through a landscaped order of sanitary surfaces.

The representation of nature as an object of 'regulated exploitation,' as a 'hygienic ghetto' that is homogenized as a commodity, is an image of nature which corporations rely on to legitimize environmentally degrading practices. This hegemonic image of nature could hardly be more vividly illustrated than in an advertisement for a Canadian printing company, celebrating the apparent success of a reforestation program carried out in cooperation with the Scouts of Canada (see Figure 15). This representation of a 'reforested landscape' is also the image of the 'abstract' space of emparked nature: perfectly shaped plantation-like trees fixed on a landscape constituted by a Stetson campaign hat, with two clouds perched above. This ideal of nature, promoted by a printing company that relies on the pulp and paper industry, is a perfect expression of the 'abstract' space of emparked nature. The image of this 'replenished resource' epitomizes the same mentalities of regulated exploitation carried out in park space: that natural resources can, quite remarkably, be both exploited and preserved. Yet, such a landscape surely is a dead, 'frozen' space, an ecological nightmare where the natural world is subordinated to the needs and values of consumerism through an emparked hygiene. Certainly, the campaign hat itself reminds us of the moral hypocrisy of corporations, who relentlessly market themselves as good 'boy scouts' of nature, while carrying out projects of resource extraction that are environmentally degrading.

While this representation of nature emparked in park jurisdictions is congruent with the exploitation of consumerism, emparked nature acts more subtly to mask environmental toxification. Ulrich Beck argues that environmental risks become both more 'real' and 'unreal': more real in the sense that they become more lethal and toxic in ways that are not even known or calculable; more unreal in the sense that they are no longer perceptible to the human senses, and essentially become invisible. This unreal, invisible character of environmental toxification can easily be manipulated and masked by absent experts who carry out emparkment practices.

The role that emparked nature plays in legitimizing environmentally destructive practices can be best understood by examining how parks dramatize the 'polluter pays principle' through the construction of tangible, situational, and individualized risks. As long as risks are individualized through legislation, as long as someone can be said to be at fault, as long a polluter can be punished and made to pay, then the multi-causal, synthetic effects

Figure 15 50 Million Trees and Still Growing (Courtesy of St Joseph's Printing, Concord, Ontario)

of toxification will remain masked. Beck (1992:31) writes: 'It is essential, however, that even in the incalculable profusion of individual interpretations, *individual conditions are again and again related to each other. Let us pick out forest destruction. So long as bark beetles, squirrels or the particular responsible forestry office were still being considered as causes and guilty parties, we were seemingly concerned not with the 'risk of modernization,' but rather with sloppy forestry or animal voracity'* (emphasis added).

Indeed, it is not hard to picture Heidegger's forester, subordinated to the orderability of a 'world of commodities,' walking down the forest path worrying about pest management or campfires. The individualization of risk through regulation constructs responsibilized park visitors: their conduct as 'customer-violators' is linked to self-protection as well as to the fate of the environment. In other words, park governance has constructed a wide assembly of potential polluters who are ever-present and who must participate in a severe form of self-regulating asceticism where the smallest act of non-compliance will offend 'nature.' The result is a bizarre, obscene sort of landscape where the public participates in recreational risks which have the effect of masking practices of widespread ecological toxification.

Thus, while ecologically toxic risks are silent and incalculable, and are revealed to the public only through the expertise of textually mediated argument, 'wild' risks constructed in parks are made up by conduct that is noisy, dirty, or somehow indecent. Among these situational, individualized risks I have described are audible and visual forms of noise (a loud stereo or loitering teenagers), places that are unclean and have 'dirt' present (a used can or a drunken body), places that are not open to supervision and inspection (a tent on a beach or a visitor without a permit). Indeed, the illustration of Montana's public use regulations (Figure 13) is a picture of a society playing 'under the volcano' of Beck's risk society, playing in a landscape where everyone is figured as a 'polluter' whose conduct threatens what is both natural and moral. The policing of these forms of pollution represents a massive act of 'symbolic detoxification,' where the natural environment can be preserved (even improved) by ordering personal conduct to conform to the clean, quiet, and hygienic. The cyclic temporal of emparkment mimics the notion of recycling deployed by practices such as recycling bottles and buying 'green products' (Wilson 1992), activities that are congruent with the win-win mentality of ecological marketing that posits a zero sum notion of waste management – a notion which views the waste itself as a commodity that can be marketed and consumed as a 'green' product. The results of such a conceptualization of time is that the consequences of global waste flows are made more difficult to comprehend. As Van Loon and Sabelis (1997:297) suggest, 'If recycling based on a cyclical-linear time is our ideal, we might falsely believe that damage can be undone, the ozone layer restored, epidemics contained, nuclear waste decontaminated and so forth.'

As 'hygienic ghettos' which follow the rhythm of the temporal of emparkment, parks reinforce the image of a non-polluted society as a 'non-society.' If parks represent what is ecologically and morally pure, then it becomes normal for society to be polluted at 'acceptable levels': emparked nature *provides a normative horizon for the toxification of society*. This is perhaps best illustrated in the legitimized presence of 'industrial parks' on the outskirts of cities, places where we expect high levels of pollution just as we expect parks to be places which are kept pollution-free. Emparked nature allows the public to wilfully participate in a landscape of emparked risks, which places the preservation of nature in a framework of consumerism. By representing environmental risks as sensual and visible, as risks that can be attributed to a specific polluter, as risks that are part of a landscape where the absence of pollution is the Utopia of a 'non-society,' then the real risks of late modernity remain profitable, manipulable, and hidden.

The Nature of Emparkment

It does seem remarkable that despite the role parks play in shaping the experience of freedom, there has been very little work carried out on the wider meanings of emparkment projects that govern everyday life. Perhaps this lack of critique is in itself evidence of the desperate way in which people today *need* to believe that there are some places which are untouched and preserved from the maelstrom of a world where 'all that is solid melts into air' as Berman (1982) suggests, quoting Marx. Parks remain the most taken for granted and unexamined regulatory forms in North American society. Even the most promising efforts to engage an emerging 'green criminology' seem to be in danger of uncritically reproducing highly reified categories such as 'the victim' in a discourse of 'crimes against the environment.'[1]

In adopting a Foucaultian-inspired approach to regulation, there is a temptation to abandon an analysis of the role that formal, centralized institutions play in legitimizing positive, normalizing, 'multiformed' power. Foucault's caution that 'law is not important' is wedded to a narrow conception of law as strictly an expression of the 'murderous splendour' of naked juridical right. By approaching 'the law' as a complex of informal and official practices and mentalities that strategize social relations, an analysis of power can be undertaken that includes and contextualizes the intentions and consequences of formal state-generated regulatory programs. This approach allows us to abandon an analysis which focuses on a regulatory effort as being 'more' or 'less' legal, and instead attend to the linkages between formal government and self-government, both of which rely on practices that moralize. Projects regulating the use of fire and alcohol in parks are distinct examples of how the governance of the self is always linked to a concern over the moral and material pollution of society.

The regulated Eden of emparked nature presents us with a contradiction that rests at the heart of the everyday experience of liberal governance: that our ability to experience freedom, permission and security increasingly relies on highly mediated and peculiar forms of moral regulation which police the conduct of the self. The spatial-temporal order of emparkment carries out a double movement which exemplifies a key characteristic of contemporary modes of power. Emparkment both totalizes and individualizes: individuals are rendered anonymous and placed into an aggregate of a population to be constituted and configured, while at the same time individual conduct is responsibilized in the most minute detail. Emparkment can be understood as one of the most ambitious spatializations of this mode of 'regulated freedom.' Emparked nature then acts as a preserve of 'moral capital' (Valverde 1994, 1998), an exhibition of normative order which plays a central role in constructing the experience of freedom and permission in everyday life.

Park governance does not just 'protect' natural landscapes – as legislative missions would have us believe – but rather has the more significant effect of 'making up' nature, of *representing* a natural and wild environment through regulatory discourses that evoke both personal and environmental risk. Personal and environmental risks are interdependent in a way that provide for a powerful moralizing effect: environmental risk is constructed through the presence and activities of people, who are in turn reflexively at risk because of the constructed 'naturalness' of the park. As a mode of power that represents nature in twentieth-century life, emparkment is characterized by four main features:

1. Emparkment is a *legislative* product, a political act which makes possible an assembly of representations which are stabilized in a particular site. Parks thus become part of the national biography of countries in defending their 'relationship' with the environment, and in providing citizens with roles with which to carry out a 'relationship' both within and outside the park.
2. Emparkment is constituted and missioned because of a perceived threat from without (society, which pollutes), but is governed also by a perceived threat from within, one represented by the presence of the customer/violator. Emparkment relies on a reflexive form of risk which hinges on a homology between the boundaries and thresholds of the body of the customer/violator and the policed thresholds of park space.
3. Emparkment is designed to be experienced in a transient way, as an experiential presentation that is constituted by thresholds designed to channel flows of people and to withstand the velocity of these flows. Emparkments are the most explicit dramatization of 'the re-cycled.'
4. Emparkment is the product of textually mediated expertise

*which stabilizes the ontological relationship between the production of
material space and the production of representational forms of this
space.* The experience of standing in a place that is seen, and
a postcard of a park scene, are united in the experience of
emparkment mediated by an immense representational
infrastructure.

While all park landscape is socially constructed as 'natural' or
'wild,' this does not mean that some landscape does not have
ecological and organic qualities. Many theorists, in attempting to
stress the social construction of nature, gloss over this distinction,
that there is indeed a difference between a mountain or a lake
and a photograph of one, and it is within this ontological gap that
the social form of an emparkment is inserted. I am not suggesting,
then, that all nature is 'constructed,' and that our present-day
forests, lakes, soil, and air are now simply products of our culture.
Such a position would be, of course, untenable. I am suggesting,
however, that as a mode of power, emparkment generates and
enforces a certain order of representation that often has nothing
to do with the rarity or ecological complexity of a specific landscape, and that this emparkment aesthetic has made it increasingly difficult to discern between spaces which are simply
manufactured and presented for human recreation and commercial exploitation, and areas which are ecologically rare and valuable. As Simon Schama (1995:9) reminds us, 'Even the landscapes
that we suppose to be most free of our culture may turn out, on
closer inspection, to be its product ... Would we rather that
Yosemite, for all its overpopulation and overrepresentation, had
never been identified, mapped, emparked' (emphasis in original).
The answer, in the first instance is, of course, no. But such an
admission does not provide an alibi for the fact that the form of
the emparkment itself, which is given great authority and majesty
by sites such as Yosemite, has in reality legitimized and masked a
wide variety of environmentally degrading and toxifying practices.
More subtly, emparkment leads us into the fallacy that the only
valuable ecological systems are those that exist in park form, a
situation which is especially disconcerting when we consider that

the greatest threats to the global ecology – the pollution of fresh and sea water, the degradation of the ozone layer, the chemical toxification of food chains, the homogenization of gene pools – lie outside the juridical protection of emparkment projects.

Once we come to see that the ways we maintain and experience 'the natural' in our lives is a direct reflection of the ordering of social relations, we will be more able to engage in *intellectually honest* efforts at park making, free from a 'commons tragedy' mindset. In an influential essay first published in 1968, Garrett Hardin outlined what he saw as 'the tragedy of the commons' – the inevitable destruction of environmental resources by public freedom of access. Hardin noted that the national parks provided a glaring examples of this, as places where the values sought by park visitors would eventually be destroyed, 'We must soon cease to treat the parks as commons,' Hardin wrote, 'or they will be of no value to anyone' (Hardin 1977:21). This outlook, marked by a social Darwinism and a political economy of an 'individualized, utility-maximizing, property owning democracy' (Harvey 1996:372) has very much epitomized the mentalities of parks managers. In order to continually justify their public mandate – increasingly under neo-liberal government regimes – park managers have allowed almost every imaginable form of recreation into parks, while at the same time putting in place intensive regulatory schemes which specifically focus on the conduct of park users. The construction of the customer-violator has been both broadened and intensified within an ever-increasing range of permitted conduct. The ever expanding range of ways we can experience nature through the experience of freedom is increasingly dependent on a more intensive ordering of the self.

By identifying and unravelling this contradiction, we are able to interrogate the central illusion which underpins the production of 'nature' governed through emparkment: the idea that we have a 'relationship' with nature. Certainly, the idea that we have such a relationship, one that can be 'healed' through the experience of park visitation, is deeply attractive to us. Even the most observant commentators on the social construction of nature (Wilson 1992) cannot seem to escape from a 'relationship' framework. This ability to experience a relationship *with* nature has become a sophisticated technique to engage in systematic and officially validated forms of pollution, a situation most recently dramatized in the 1997 Earth Summit in New York, where widespread forms of global pollution were rationalized within the zero sum rationale of 'carbon trading.'

Once we shift away from this idea that we have a 'relationship' with nature through the order of emparkment, we can attend to how the natural spaces of parks are constituted primarily through the ordering of social relations. *Whenever we talk about having a 'relationship' with nature, what we are really speaking of is the specific ordering of relations between people, and, more specifically, the ordering of 'the conduct of the self.'* The social construction of nature, and the constructed nature of social relations as being normal and acceptable, are intimately linked. Carolyn Merchant has vividly illustrated how the organic cosmology of the world, undermined by the scientific revolution and patriarchal rationalism in the sixteenth and seventeenth centuries, was brought about by the disciplining and exploitation of nature and the subordination and control of women, who so powerfully symbolized this organic disorder. The shift from an organic cosmos to a mechanistic model of nature has marked the managerial techniques of resource management which emparkment order relies upon: to challenge the construction of women as culturally passive and subordinate is also to challenge the mechanist view of dominated nature (Merchant 1989). We do not have to look far to see the horrible end to which such a view of nature has been deployed: to carry out the genocide of the Second World War, the head of the SS, Heinrich Himmler, evoked a 'culture in awe of nature' that would bind 'blood and soil' (Pelt 1994:101–5). In dealing with the 'Jewish problem' in Poland, Himmler visualized a sanitized landscape of planted trees and hedges that would work in such unison that even rainfall could be controlled to secure plentiful harvests (103).

By moving away from the idea of carrying out a relationship with nature through emparkment order, we can also begin to rethink an illusory distinction between the country and the city. As Williams (1973) discusses in one of his best works, *The Country and the City*, this distinction is an illusion which denigrates the city and romanticizes the country, one which reaffirms the idea of nature as a destination that can be travelled to as an escape from city life. This distinction powerfully evokes the idea of city polluters who can be 'made to pay' through proper conduct within country and park settings. Certainly, emparkment remains a model for governing urban spaces, both in the idea of wildness and nature parks represent, and in the techniques of order which organize park space and regulate visitor conduct. In urban space, programs of 'civic sanitation' that clean up the visibly indigent such as the homeless increasingly rely on a social imagination dominated by the metaphor of wildness and wilderness, and, particularly in the United States, the notion of a frontier which can be conquered (Smith 1996). The result has been a 'hardening' of public space (Davis 1998), which moralizes and excludes those who offend against a civilized 'quality of life.'

In arguing for the 'uses of disorder,' Richard Sennett (1970: 130) argues that such attempts to sanitize public spaces can have disturbing consequences with regard to the way people relate to one another; that the vast lonely 'jungle' of the city can provide a challenging social matrix characterized by diversity and complex experience. Yet, it is precisely this character of 'planned anarchy' advocated by Sennett which parks have occupied in the public imagination for most of this century. For the link between disorder and freedom has emerged as the central theme in the governance of the everyday within late modern life, a contradiction which is nowhere more vividly dramatized then in the nature of emparked order.

Knotless Wood

The image of a disciplined nature evoked by the woodyard customer's request for knotless wood represents an authoritarian sensibility, where any anomaly or imperfection is wiped out. A forest of knotless trees might produce firewood that has few sparks and telephone poles and lumber that are perfectly grained, but such a forest would also be an ecological nightmare of homogeneity where no birds sing. The park customer's request for knotless wood is a powerful metaphor for emparkment and for the ways in which 'nature' has been organized as a political object in modern life. More fundamentally, the request for knotless wood is representative of an impulse to moral order which attempts to police impurity and dissent, a form of order which underpins the ways in which nature is constituted through emparkment strategies.

It would be unfortunate if readers see this book as unduly pessimistic concerning the future of parks and the possibility for resistance and change. My suggestion that we must rethink the idea that we have a 'relationship' with emparked nature, while counter-intuitive to most of us, is necessary if we are to seriously address questions concerning environmental toxification and destruction. In order to forge an alternative in environmental politics, we must resist the idea that we can 'return to nature' or even 'step outside' it (Cronon 1995). We must stop thinking of nature as the 'other,' as something outside of ourselves that can be mysteriously accessed if only we hike in enough parks or rinse enough bottles for our Blue Boxes. And, as I have stressed, the realization of how the experience of 'the natural' is manufactured in parks does not mean that ecological and organic landscapes and features are not real, nor that our reactions to emparked spectacles are feigned or insignificant. Indeed, the very fact that we feel stirred and moved by nature emparkments in a collective way seems even more reason to take parks seriously as regulated sites of freedom, an even stronger reason to understand how the places that we often feel are most natural are in fact constituted by the most human means.

Notes

Chapter 1: The Emparkment of Nature

1 See, for example, Hunt and Wickham (1994), Rose (1990), Dean (1991), and Valverde (1998).

2 Foucaultian scholar Mitchell Dean (1991:12) describes government as 'a general term which includes any relatively calculated practice to direct categories of social agents in a particular manner and to specified ends.'

3 For a more general discussion, see Ericson and Haggerty (1997: 156–76) on insurential technologies in policing.

4 For a detailed discussion of the establishment of North American parks, see Ise (1961), Sellars (1997), and Runte (1990).

5 See Olmsted's *Public Parks and the Enlargement of Towns* (1970) as well as his collected papers entitled 'Creating Central Park' (Olmsted 1983), for his vision of urban parks that would combat the immoral environment of 'town life.'

6 Emparkment projects closely aligned with imperial power did not just occur on a grand scale. At Oxford the university parks estate, founded in 1854, played an important role in the leisure and sporting activities of an institution that was at the centre of imperial rule. Certainly, the expression of gentlemanly outdoor pursuits has perhaps been most notably carried out through the Boy Scout movement, a group Edward Said (1993: 166) describes as 'bright-eyed, eager and resourceful little middle class servants of empire.'

Chaper 2: The Ranger Mission

1 For example, at the federal level in the United States, firetower rangers are

employed by the United States Forestry Service, while park rangers are employees of the National Parks Service.

2 See Shields (1991: 184–5) on the notion of langscape.

3 I will retain the use of the descriptor 'park ranger' to describe both American and Canadian emparkment agents, and will draw attention to the warden character of Canadian agents when instructive.

4 As far as I am aware, the only jurisdictions that use the title 'park police' are the United States Park Police stationed at two of the five 'urban' parks under the NPS umbrella.

5 For example, 'All Provincial parks are dedicated to the people of Ontario' (Ontario A:s.2).

6 Other examples include 'and the purpose of parks ... is to provide for public enjoyment of the same in a way that will leave them unimpaired and minimize conflict among users' (Minnesota C:s.6100.0200). For other examples, see Nova Scotia (B), Colorado (C), Oregon (A:7), Illinois (A:s.3(1)), Louisiana (A:s.101(1)), Nebraska (B:s.001:1), Delaware (A:s1-1), Georgia (D:s.5.391.5.01), Tennessee (A: s.5.0400-2-1-.01), New Jersey (D:s.7:2-2.1), Ontario (A:s.2)

7 For example: (Colorado, C:s.33-1-101; emphasis added). See also Delaware (A:s.1.1), where authorities are mandated to 'protect park resources and improvements thereto.'

8 See also Oklahoma (A:p.112) and Michigan (A).

9 The use of the title 'ranger' by Alberta and British Columbia are the only exceptions I have found to the usual Canadian title, 'warden.'

10 These passages are a reminder of how close law enforcement mentalities in general are tied to notions of ownership and private property.

11 While it is certainly true that American Rangers are armed while Canadian wardens are not, many American rangers do not carry sidearms at all.

12 With two exceptions, all jurisdictions under examination provide their rangers with some sort of designation as law enforcement officers. Vermont and Indiana are the only two that simply utilize 'security' staff who are civilians (see Vermont A; Indiana B).

13 University and transport 'police' forces in Canada provide examples of other agencies that, while initially deployed to provide an alternative to police services, end up with 'piggybacked' authorities in a way that apes police practices.

14 See Hutter (1997:12) on the notion of compliance in regulatory discourses; in particular see Hawkins (1984) on how compliance to pollution abatement legislation is negotiated.

15 As echoed in two of the most popular self-regulatory slogans connected
with recreation: 'ONLY YOU can prevent drinking and driving,' and 'ONLY YOU
can prevent forest fires.'

16 See also Colorado (S.33-10-106)

17 For example, in the year 1994, the Kansas Parks Enforcement summary
reports a total permit compliance rate of 97.25%.

Chapter 3: Regulating Park Space

1 For other notable examples, see Nova Scotia (A:s.8(1)(a)), South Dakota
(A:s.41-04-01-02), Indiana (A:407.063), Northwest Territories (A:s.3(1)),
Alberta (C:11(2)).

2 For similar but less ambitious definitions see, for example, Oklahoma
(A:s.725:30-2-4) and Utah (H:s.R651-601-9).

3 For example, Yukon (A:s.1) utilizes the following designations for park
types: 'recreation park,' 'historic park,' and 'natural environment park.'

4 See also Vermont (B) and Montana (A:s.II (d)) for a classification of
'primitive' campsites.

5 For other typical examples, see Georgia (D:s.391-5 -2-.02 (r)) and Washington (B:WAC 352-32-053).

6 The importance of trail makers in providing comfort and accessibility has
been given special emphasis by the widespread movement to make park
experiences accessible to those who are physically handicapped. Picnic
tables are designed to be high enough for wheelchair use, Braille is used on
trail markers and interpretive plaques, and activities such as hunting are
modified for disabled participation.

7 Of interest here is the official graffiti used to mark lookout points. As
depicted in Figure 7, this often involves the image of a camera, or of an
adult looking through binoculars at a spectacle being pointed to by a child.

8 The other nursery story that comes to mind is 'Little Red Riding Hood,'
which emphasizes both the importance of the path and the dangers (especially for women) of travelling alone in the wilderness. See Opie and Opie
(1974: 119–22, 308–19) for translations and discussion of these famous
forest stories.

Chapter 4: The Regulation of Conduct

1 Other notable examples: '"Camp" or "camping" means the use of a shelter
such as a tent, trailer, motor vehicle, tarpaulin, bedroll or sleeping bag for

temporary residence or sleeping purposes' (Wisconsin A:s. NR 45.03(4));
'"Camping" means ... the arrangement of bedding for the purpose of, or in
such a way as will permit, remaining overnight' (Indiana A:s.407.0065);
'"Camping" means the temporary placing of a tent, shelter, lean-to, sleeping bag, bedding material ... for sleeping overnight in an outdoor setting'
(New Jersey A:s.7:2-1.7). Campsites are routinely defined in terms of
'camping units'; in Montana a camping unit is defined as 'any device
designed for sleeping' (Montana A:s. II(A)).

2 Like every other aspect of park experience, camping is considered a
  transient activity; widespread prohibitions prevent park users from taking
  up residency, and time limits are often established restricting the number
  of days a camper can stay.

3 Thus, a group of teenage couples would be restricted to three couples a
  site, while exceptions would be made for larger groups who are related to
  one another through marriage.

4 For example: 'Occupancy of a site is limited to one family unit or a group
  of no more then five persons per site. A responsible person of 18 years of
  age or older shall accompany each group' (Pennsylvania, F:s.31.33.)

5 'Rangers are being thrust into activities that require managing visitor
  behaviour ... The enforcement role of the park ranger is a very positive and
  necessary element ensuring that the depreciative behaviour of a few does
  not deter the many others from enjoying their outdoor recreational experience' (Alberta, J:1).

6 Another example: 'For a person commits disorderly conduct when with
  intent to cause public alarm, nuisance, jeopardy or violence, or knowingly
  and recklessly creating a risk thereof such person ... [E]ngages in fighting
  or threatening, or in violent behaviour' (Oklahoma, A: 725:30-4-17).

7 Another notable example: 'No person shall operate any sound truck,
  loudspeaker, generator, chainsaw, air conditioner, or other device that
  produces excessive, loud or unusual noises without first obtaining a written
  permit from the department' (Wisconsin A:s.3(2)(e)).

8 For example, 'The department may establish quiet zones by posted notice.
  Within quiet zones, no person may operate a radio, boombox, musical
  instrument, tape player or similar noise producing device, unless the noise
  is confined to the person through the use of a headset' (Wisconsin A:s.3
  (2)(l)).

9 For other notable examples of the deployment of a 'reasonably prudent
  person,' see Georgia (D:s.391-5-1-.05), Oklahoma (A:s.725:30-4-6, 725:30-4-
  7) and New Jersey (A:s.7:2–2.11).

10 The gender of discursive personages present in regulatory discourses is a fascinating issue, albeit one that I will not pursue here.

11 Even in the context of an indecent criminal act, legislators still find it necessary to draw a distinction between 'normal' and 'deviant' sexual behaviour, even though they would both constitute an offence.

12 See also Pennsylvania (F:s 31.92).

13 For example, in New Jersey (A:s.7:2-2.11 (m)); 'A person shall not loiter in or about any comfort station or other public structure'; in Georgia (D:s. 391-5-1-.05 (10) 'no person over the age of five years shall enter into or loiter near any site, structure, or section thereof reserved and designated for exclusive use by the opposite sex'; and in California (B:s.4318) 'no person shall loiter, prowl or wander about a park restroom, shower or changing facility and peek into the doors and windows.'

14 Another notable example reads: 'The use of drinking fountains, springs, lakes, or waterways for washing purposes is prohibited' (Pennsylvania, F:s.31.39).

15 Although, as I have discussed, many of the regulations imply that park authorities cannot even count on humans to defecate in the proper locations!

16 Widespread exemptions are present that allow people with Seeing Eye dogs or guide dogs to enter public places such as restaurants, offices, and beaches.

17 Other notable examples include Florida (A:s.16D-2.004 (1)(g)), South Carolina (A:s.1(p)), Nova Scotia (A:s.24(1)(2)(3)(4), Vermont (B:s.5(1)(2)(3)), Michigan (A:s.R299.324 (a)(b)), Pennsylvania (F:s.31.11(a)(b)), California (B:ss.4312(a)(b)(c)(d)(e)), Oregon (A:s.OAR 736-10-030 (1)(2)(3)(4)(5)(6)(7)).

18 For example, 'No person shall feed or attempt to pet any wild animal' (Florida, A:160-2:0037(b)). See also British Columbia (B:s.30) and Parks Canada (A:p.10).

19 For an excellent discussion of the MADD movement, see Reinarman (1988).

20 The campaign against drunk driving has been so strong that it has provided a general framework from within which moral panic is easily manufactured. For example, the recent moral panic over unsafe truck drivers during the 1995 Ontario provincial election could not have been carried out without implicitly evoking the reckless character of the drunk driver, with which truck drivers were associated in the public mindset. More recently, the former Canadian federal justice minister, Alan Rock, in announcing a

crackdown on men who refuse to pay child support, told reporters that 'deadbeat dads' should 'be considered on the same plane as drunk drivers.'

21 A significant difference between Canadian and American legislation is that American legislation tends to regulate alcohol use within park legislation, while Canadian jurisdictions rely specifically on liquor acts to regulate alcohol. The same can be said to a lesser degree for questions of conduct.

22 For example, 'Without a doubt, the greatest majority of the problems within Alberta Parks and Recreation areas results from the over indulgence of alcohol' (Alberta, D); other examples include New Jersey (B), Michigan (A), Kansas (A), Northwest Territories (C), and Missouri (B).

23 For typical examples see Nevada (B) and South Dakota, (A).

24 For example, 'Parks close to urban areas are more heavily used and as a result more liquor related problems are experienced' (Nova Scotia C); and 'Most of the [liquor] violations occur within parks located near the City of St Louis, which is the most heavily populated area in Missouri' (B).

25 For example: 'We may utilize local or state enforcement agencies in conjunction with our employees to perform special "enforcement" efforts ... from DUI check lanes to use of specially trained dogs for detection of illegal substances' (Kansas, A).

26 Other examples of the construction of the alcohol problem based on the failure of regulatory efforts: 'The most numerous violation is the possession or consumption of alcoholic beverages which is prohibited by law' (North Carolina A), and 'Alcohol and alcohol related incidents are very common as alcoholic beverages are prohibited in all state parks and forests' (New Jersey A).

27 This technique, which was used on a limited basis at several parks in southwestern Ontario, epitomizes legal incompetence. Any park official who would arbitrarily refuse anyone entry to a public park because he or she did not agree to forfeit their constitutional right to protection from unreasonable search and seizure would risk serious civil action.

28 The burning oil drum has become a familiar fixture on the picket lines during labour disputes.

29 Thus, in the context of forest fire prevention, the definition of smoking includes the carrying around of a lighted object, not just inhalation. For example, in Georgia smoking is defined as 'the carrying of lighted cigarettes, cigars or pipes, or the intentional and direct inhalation of smoke from these objects.'

30 For example, 'A fire shall be continuously under the surveillance of a competent individual 16 years old or older. A fire shall be extinguished before the responsibility of the permittee ends' (Maryland A:.10).

31 For a discussion of the often controversial methods used to exhibit and manage bears in park settings, see Sellars (1997: 249–52) and Runte (1990: 223–4).

Chapter 5: The Emparkment of Order

1 See, for example, the special issue of *Theoretical Criminology*, 1998, 2(2), which focuses on 'Green Criminology.'

References

STATE AND PROVINCIAL SOURCES

Note: Sources are referenced here and in text by jurisdiction (e.g., Alabama), item (e.g., A), and, where appropriate, section or page numbers (e.g., s.220-5-.01).

The United States

Alabama (State of)

A. 'Alabama Rules and Regulations for State Parks' (s.220-5-.01 to 220-5-.16).
B. Correspondence, 14 Sept. 1994, Marcus S. Easterwood, Supervisor, Operations and Maintenance. State of Alabama Department of Conservation and Natural Resources.

California (State of)

A. Correspondence, 20 June 1995, Stephen P. O'Brien, Superintendent, Law Enforcement. State of California Department of Parks and Recreation.
B. 'Title XIV California Code of Regulations.' Div. 3, Department of Parks and Recreation. (June 1992): 431-68.
C. 'Fatal Accidents in Park Units 1993,' Breakdown of Accidents by Cause.

Colorado (State of)

A. Correspondence. 31 July 1995. Rick Storm, Chief of Law Enforcement, Colorado State Parks.

B. 'Code of Colorado Regulations.' Chap. 1: Parks and Outdoor Recreation Lands, 16 CR11:11-93; chap. 2: Boating; chap. 3: River Outfitters, 18 CR 6: 6–95; chap. 4: Snowmobile Regulations; chap. 5: Off-Highway Vehicle Regulations, 14 CR, 5-91; chap. 6: Procedural Rules.

C. 'Title 33' Parks and Wildlife Statutes: Articles 1–44 and related Statutes, including General Provisions; Non-Game and End Species; Damage by Wildlife; Licences and Fees; Protection of Fish Streams; Law Enforcement and Penalties; Recreational Trails; Passes and Registrations; Arkansas River Recreational Act; Vessels; Snowmobiles; Off-Highway Vehicles; Colorado Natural areas; Ski Safety; and Liability.

D. Brochures 1995. *Land and Water Regulations*; *Boating Statutes and Regulations*; *Snowmobile Facts and Regulations*; '*Off-Highway Vehicle Information*; *Colorado State Parks Guide*.

E. Statistics for years 90/91 and 91/92: Uniform Crime Report Summary; Citations Issued data; Parks Law Violations; Wildlife Law Violations; Traffic Law violations; Criminal Code Violations (Title 18 & 21) Non-Alcohol-Related; Criminal Code Violations (Title 18 & 12) Alcohol-Related; Comparisons of Lakes and Rivers; Recreational Boating Accident Statistics (property damage, personal injuries, fatalities).

Delaware (State of)

A. 'Delaware State Park Rules and Regulations.' Department of Natural Resources and Environmental Control, Delaware Division of Parks and Recreation pursuant to Title 7. 'Delaware Code,' chap. 47, subsection 4702 (c).

B. Correspondence. 2 Sept. 1994. Gregory L. Wilson, Enforcement of Safety Administration. State of Delaware Department of Natural Resources and Environmental Control, Division of Parks and Recreation.

Florida (State of)

A. Title 16, Department of Natural Resources transferred to Title 62, Department of Environmental Protection. Chap. 16D-2, 'Operation of Division Recreation Areas and Facilities.'

B. Correspondence. 6 Sept. 1994, Lt. Colonel Joe R. Henderson, Jr., Chief, Bureau of Florida Park Patrol, Department of Environmental Protection.

C. 'Sign Catalog, Division of Recreation and Parks.' Rev. Feb. 1997.

Georgia (State of)

A. Georgia Game and Fish and Boat Safety Act. 1992 ed.

B. March 1993. Parks, Recreation and Historic Sites Division Law Enforcement Procedure.
C. '1800 Law Enforcement (operating procedures).'
D. 'Rules of Georgia Department of Natural Resources,' Parks, Recreation and Historic Sites, Chap. 391-1-1, State Parks and Historic Sites System.
E. Correspondence. 14 Sept. 1994. Wayne Escoe, Ass't. Chief of Operations, Georgia Department of Natural Resources.

Hawaii (State of)

A. Chap. 184, Hawaii Revised Statues, State Parks and Recreation Areas.
B. Correspondence. 30 Aug. 1994. Ralston H. Nagata, State Parks Administrator, State of Hawaii Department of Lands and Natural Resources.

Illinois (State of)

A. Title 17. Conservation, Chap. 1; Department of Conservation Subchap A: Lands and Historic Sites, pt. 110. 'Public Use of State Parks and Other Properties of the Department of Conservation.'
B. Correspondence. 18 Aug. 1994. James Prudon, Illinois Department of Conservation.

Indiana (State of)

A. '310 IAC 4.5-1-1, Department of Natural Resources, Art. 5. 'General Use Regulations,' Department of Land and Water Areas.
B. Correspondence. 27 Aug. 1994. John Bergman, Assistant Director, Division of State Parks, State of Indiana Department of Natural Resources.

Iowa (State of)

A. 'Code of Iowa,' 461A.1, Public Lands and Waters.
B. 'Regulations for Iowa State Parks and Recreation Areas.'
C. Correspondence. 19 Sept. 1994. Jim Scheffler, Executive Officer II, Parks, Recreation and Preserves Division, Iowa Department of Natural Resources.

Kansas (State of)

A. Correspondence, 12 June 1995. Mark E. Johnson. Parks Assistant Director, Operations Office, Department of Wildlife and Parks.
B. 'Customer Service Evaluation.' Kansas Wildlife and Parks.

C. 'Public Lands Regulations Summary,' 115-2-2 to 115-18-5. 06/93.
D. 'Parks Enforcement 1994 Annual Summary.'
E. Statutes 32-808 to 32-1051, Wildlife, Parks and Recreation; Statutes 115-8-1 to 115-8-21, Department of Lands and Waters.

Louisiana (State of)

A. Louisiana Office of State Parks. 'Rules and Regulations.' Rev. 1993. Department of Culture, Recreation and Tourism.
B. Correspondence, 12 Sept. 1994, Randall G. Trahan, Chief of Park Operations. State of Louisiana, Department of Culture, Recreation and Tourism.
C. Correspondence. 8 Aug. 1995. Randy Trahan, Chief of Operations, State of Louisiana Department of Culture, Recreation and Tourism.

Maine (State of)

A. Bureau of Parks and Recreation, 04-059, Maine Department of Conservation, chap. 1: 'Rules for State Parks and Historic Sites.'
B. Chapter 203, Bureau of Parks and Recreation.

Maryland (State of)

A. Natural Resources article, 'title 5, subtitle 206, title 08,' Department of Natural Resources, subtitle 07, Forests and Parks.
B. Various public relations material, including 'Park Watch,' 'Trash Free Parks,' and 'Growing, Not Mowing' literature.
C. Correspondence, 30 Aug. 1994. Lt. Christopher Bushman, Ass't. Chief, Field Operations. State of Maryland Department of Natural Resources.

Massachusetts (State of)

A. 304 CMR: Division of Forests and Parks, 304 CMR 12:00: 'General Prohibitions.'
B. Commonwealth of Massachusetts, Department of Environmental Management, Division of Forests and Parks, *Park Ranger Program Manual.*'
C. Correspondence. 13 Sept. 1994. Todd A. Frederick, Director, Commonwealth of Massachusetts, Department of Environmental Management.

Michigan (State of)

A. Correspondence. 22 Aug. 1994. John Winters, Law/Training Section, Parks and Recreation Division, State of Michigan Department of Natural Resources.

B. Handouts. 'Notice – Alcoholic Beverage Ban'; 'A Guide for Visitors with Pets.'
C. 'Law Enforcement – General Policy,' Michigan State Parks System Act 149, 1960.
D. Department of Natural Resources, Parks Division State Parks and Recreation Areas: R299.321 to R299.328.
E. 'Land Use Orders of the Director.' By authority conferred on the Director of the Department of Natural Resources. Section 3a of Act 17 of the Public Acts of 1921, as amended.

Minnesota (State of)

A. Correspondence. 12 July 1995. Dan Breva, Operation Co-ordinator, Division of Parks and Recreation, Minnesota Department of Natural Resources.
B. Statute Sections 85.04 to 86A.06.
C. 'Sign Manual.' Minnesota Department of Natural Resources.

Missouri (State of)

A. 'Missouri's Masterpiece – State Parks and Historic Sites,' Missouri Department of Natural Resources.
B. Correspondence. 14 June 1995. Major Ernest G. McCutchen, Missouri State Park Rangers, State of Missouri Department of Natural Resources, Division of State Parks.
C. Ranger 1993 Incident Summary; State Summary. Missouri Department of Natural Resources, Division of State Parks.
D. Missouri Department of Natural resources, Organizational Chart, Regions I, III.
E. '*State Park Laws of Missouri: A Handbook for Park Rangers,*' by Walter E. Busch, 1993.

Montana (State of)

A. *A Guide to Montana's Public Use Regulations.* State of Montana, Department of Fish, Wildlife and Parks, Final 1994/95/96 Biennial Fee Rule – State Park System User Fees.
B. Parks Title 23, Parks, Recreation, Sports and Gambling. Chap. 1: Parks.

Nebraska (State of)

A. Nebraska State statutes 81-801, Independent Boards and Commissions, Nebraska Game and Parks Commission.

B. 'Title 163,' Nebraska Administrative Code. 'Rules and Regulations Concerning Parks.' Chap. 5. Nebraska Game and Parks Commission,
C. Correspondence, 24 Aug. 1994. James Fuller, Division Administrator, Nebraska Game and Parks Commission.
D. 'A Brief History of the Games and Parks Commission.'
E. Article 11, Park Entry Permits Section 37-1101-37-1114.
F. Game and Parks Commission 81-801: 729–47.
G. Law Enforcement, Nebraska Game and Parks Commission. No. 01-11-01, 'Firearms Policy,' effective 10 Oct. 1993. Distribution to all conservation officers.

Nevada (State of)

A. Nevada Administrative Code 407, State Parks and Monuments.
B. Correspondence, 6 Sept. 1994. Steven B. Silva, Division Law Enforcement Coordinator, State of Nevada, Department of Conservation and Natural Resources, Division of State Parks.

New Jersey (State of)

A. 'Rules and Regulations' (State Park Service Code). Department of Environmental Protection, Division of Parks and Forestry. New Jersey.
B. Correspondence. 13 Sept. 1994. Richard F. Barker, Assistant Director, State Park Service. State of New Jersey Department of Environmental Protection, Division of Parks and Forestry.
C. Correspondence, 10 Aug. 1995. Richard F. Barker, Assistant Director, State Park Service. State of New Jersey Department of Environmental Protection, Division of Parks and Forestry.
D. New Jersey *State Park Service Monthly Activity Report: 1994 Year End Totals.*
E. *Sign Manual* New Jersey State Park Service. Rev. 5 June 1997.

New Mexico (State of)

A. New Mexico State Parks. 1994. *Summary of Fees and Regulations.*
B. 'New Mexico State Parks – Discover the Enchantment' Doc. 081991.

North Carolina (State of)

A. Chaps. 14 and 15B of the North Carolina General Statutes, 113-34 and 113-35, 113-28.1.

B. Correspondence. 9 Sept. 1994. James B. Hallsey, State of North Carolina Department of Environment, Health and Natural Resources.

North Dakota (State of)

A. North Dakota Park Use Rules – North Dakota State Parks.
B. North Dakota Administrative Code. Chaps. 58-02-08 and 55-08: 'Parks and Recreation Department'; chap. 39-24: 'Regulation and Registration of Snowmobiles'; chap. 39-00 'All-Terrain Vehicles.'
C. Correspondence, 29 Aug. 1994. Don Underwood, Chief of Park Operations, North Dakota Parks and Recreation Department.
D. Correspondence. 4 Aug. 1995. Don Underwood, Chief of Park Operations. North Dakota Parks and Recreation Department.
E. *'Seasonal Ranger Training' Manual.*
F. 'Park Use Rules – North Dakota Administrative Code. Chaps. 58-02-08, effective 1 July 1994.
G. '1995 State Park Fees.'

Oklahoma (State of)

A. 'Oklahoma Tourism and Recreation Department Operating Procedure Number P10-5-300.' *Ranger's Manual and Addendum Procedures.'*

Oregon (State of)

A. Oregon Revised Statues 390 Series. Oregon Parks and Recreation Department, 'Park Area Rules and Enforcement Guidelines.' June 1994, including chap. 736, div. 10, General Park Area Rules.
B. Correspondence. 14 Sept. 1994, Mary K. Bachurin, Coordinator, Safety, Law Enforcement, Training. Oregon Parks and Recreation Department.

Pennsylvania (State of)

A. Administrative Code of 1929, s. 1906.
B. Correspondence. 30 Aug. 1994. Commonwealth of Pennsylvania Department of Environmental Resources.
C. Correspondence. 31 Aug. 1995. Commonwealth of Pennsylvania Department of Environmental Resources.
D. 'Summary of Pennsylvania State Area Rules and Regulations,' 6000- FS-DERO502.
E. Pennsylvania State Park Incident Summaries, 1993, 1994.

F. 'Pennsylvania State Parks Rules and Regulations for State Recreation Areas,' DER-#267-6/92.

South Carolina (State of)

A. 'State Park Rules and Regulations' (R566, H2740).

South Dakota (State of)

A. *Use of Parks and Public Lands*. Chap. 41:03:01.
B. *South Dakota Park Times*. 1994.
C. State Statutes. Series 41-15 to 41-17.
D. Correspondence. 15 Sept. 1994. South Dakota Department of Game, Fish and Parks.

Tennessee (State of)

A. Tennessee Department of Conservation, Tennessee State Parks, *Rules and Regulations Governing the Use of Tennessee State Parks*. Chap. 0400-2-1: General; chap. 0400-2-2: 'Public Use And Recreation'; chap. 0400-2-3: 'Boating'; chap. 0400-2-4: 'Marina Operations.'
B. Handout *Tennessee State Parks*.
C. Correspondence, 4 Aug. 1995, Bill Boswell, Assistant Director, State of Tennessee Department of Environment and Conservation.
D. Correspondence. 24 Aug. 1994. Bill Boswell, Assistant Director, State of Tennessee Department of Environment and Conservation.

Utah (State of)

A. *Know Before You Go: Utah's Off-Highway Vehicle Education Student Workbook*, 2d ed., rev. Apriul 1993. State of Utah Natural Resources, Division of Parks and Recreation.
B. *Utah Boating Basics: A Guide to Responsible Boating*, 1-2 UT BB 14951.
C. *Utah Division of Parks and Recreation 1994 Status Report*. State of Utah Natural Resources, 325/195.
D. 'Highlights from Utah Off-Highway Vehicle Laws and Rules,' 7/89.
E. *Utah State Parks! Discover the Diversity*, rev. Jan. 1994.
F. 'Highlights from Utah Boating Law and Rules,' rev. 6/94 120M.
G. 'Utah Off-Highway Vehicle Act and Board of Parks and Recreation' Rules. Title 41, chap. 22. Utah Code. Annotated 1953; amended Jan. 1992.
H. 'State Park Rules.' Authorized by Parks and Recreation Act, title 63, chap. 11. Utah Code, annotated Aug. 1992.

I. 'Utah Boating Act and Board of Parks and recreation Rules,' title 73, chapter 18, Utah Code, annotated 1953, updated March 1993.

J. Correspondence. 15 Aug. 1995. Jay Christianson, Park Operations Coordinator, State of Utah Department of Natural Resources, Division of Parks and Recreation.

K. *Sign Handbook.* 1 May 1991. Utah Natural Resources Parks and Recreation.

Vermont (State of)

A. Correspondence. 15 Nov. 1995. Edward J. Koenemann, Director of State Parks and Recreation, State of Vermont Agency of Natural Resources.

B. '1994 Rules and Regulations, Vermont Department of Forests, Parks and Recreation.' Adopted 14 Dec. 1993; effective 1 Jan. 1994.

C. *Vermont State Parks Sign Manual.*

Virginia (State of)

A. Correspondence. 26 June 1995. Joe Elton, Director, Commonwealth of Virginia, Department of Conservation and Recreation.

B. *Virginia Department of Conservation and Recreation Incident Report,* 154/ C19849/1-95.

C. Code of Virginia, art. 1, State Parks 10.1 -200.

D. 'Virginia State Park Regulations.' Commonwealth of Virginia, Department of Conservation and Recreation, Division of State Parks. Adopted 6 Dec. 1979; effective 15 Jan. 1980.

Washington (State of)

A. Correspondence, 11 Aug. 1995, Kathryn J. Smith, Assistant Director of Operations, Washington State Parks and Recreation Division.

B. *Public Use of State Park Areas.* Chap. 352-32 WAC (1995 ed).

C. Commission Policy 91-60-1 Law Enforcement.

D. Chap. 43.51 Parks and Recreation Division.

E. *Sign Manual,* 1979. 2d. rev. Washington State Parks and Recreation Commission.

West Virginia (state of)

A. Correspondence. 30 Aug. 1994. Robert L. Mathis, District Administrator, West Virginia Parks and Recreation.

B. Handout: 'West Virginia, 1995: It's You.'

Wisconsin (State of)

A. *State Parks and State Forests, Miscellaneous.* Chap. NR 45. State of Wisconsin Statutes 23, 26, 27. State of Wisconsin Department of Natural Resources.
B. Correspondence. 25 Aug. 1994. Norman Pazderski, Employee Development Coordinator, Bureau of Parks and Recreation, State of Wisconsin Department of Natural Resources.
C. Correspondence. 9 Aug. 1995. Norman Pazderski, Law Enforcement Chief, State of Wisconsin Department of Natural Resources.

Canada

(Parks Canada)

A. *Sign Manual.* Canadian Parks Service, Minister of Supply and Services Canada.
B. *Trail Manual.* 1978. Canadian Parks Service, Minister of Supply and Services Canada, QS 7053-000-BB-A1.

Alberta (Province of)

A. 'The Park Law Enforcer.'
B. Provincial Parks Act. Chap. P-22 of 1980 Revised Statutes of Alberta.
C. Alberta Regulation 102/85. Provincial Parks Act, General Regulation.
D. Correspondence. 19 July 1994. G.R. Kendall, Public Safety and Security Coordinator, Alberta Environmental Protection, Parks Services.
E. Correspondence. 12 Oct. 1995. G.R. Kendall, Alberta Environmental Protection.
F. Seasonal Park Ranger Enforcement Training, Environmental Training Centre, Hinton, 1–5, May 1995.
G. Poster: 'Welcome, Enjoy Your Stay at Alberta's Provincial Parks and Recreation Areas.'
H. Park tabloid: *Crimson Lake Provincial Park Times.* 1995 ed.
I. Park tabloid: *Long Lake Provincial Park Times* (Summer 1994).
J. *1988/89 Annual Summary, Security Service Management Information System.* (Sept. 1989) Alberta Recreation and Parks, Provincial Parks Service, Security Service Unit.

British Columbia (Province of)

A. *Public Safety, Park Security: 1993 Annual Report.* Province of British Columbia.

B. B.C. Reg. 180/90 O.C. 867/90. Park and Recreation Area Regulation Park Act. R.S. Chap. 309.
C. Correspondence. 30 Aug. 1994. R.B. Harris, Safety and Security Officer, Province of British Columbia Ministry of Environment, Lands and Parks.
D. *Public Safety Park Security: 1994 Annual Report*. Province of British Columbia.
E. Correspondence. 12 Oct. 1995. R.B. Harris, Safety and Security Officer, Province of British Columbia Ministry of Environment, Lands and Parks.
F. Park Act, R5 chap. 309, 1989.

Niagara Parks Commission (Ontario)

A. The Niagara Parks Act. R.S.O. 1990, chap. N3.
B. Correspondence. 8 Aug. 1994. D.W. Schafer, General Manager, Niagara Parks Commission.

Newfoundland and Labrador

A. Provincial Parks Regulations (amended 1961, 1963, 1966–7, 1969, 1975–6, 1978, 1980, 1983, 1985, 1987, 1991–3).
B. Chap. P-32, An Act Respecting Provincial Parks Amended 1992, c14, s1.
C. An Act to Provide for Natural Areas in the Province to Be Set Aside for the Benefit, Education and Enjoyment of the People of the Province. Chap. W-9.
E. *Provincial Parks Trail and Planning Design Manual*. April 1993. Department of Tourism and Culture.

Northwest Territories

A. The Territorial Parks Regulations, R.R.N.W.T. 1980, reg. 278. Amended by instruments numbered R-078-81, R-040-82, and R-036-83. Regulation no. 278.
B. An Act Respecting Parks in the Northwest Territories, June 1987.
C. Correspondence. N.d. Robin Reilly, Director, Parks and Visitor Services, Northwest Territories Economic Development and Tourism.
D. Correspondence. 13 Oct. 1995. Ron Seale, Special Advisor, Northwest Territories Economic Development and Tourism.
E. 'GNWT Parks Policy Discussion Paper.' Jan. 1995. Prepared to obtain public comment prior to developing a formal policy, by Parks and Visitor Services Division, Department of Economic Development and Tourism, Government of Northwest Territories.

Nova Scotia (Province of)

A. 'The Provincial Parks Act Regulations.' Made pursuant to the provisions of chap. 18 of the Statutes of Nova Scotia 1988. The Provincial Parks Act Respecting Provincial Parks.
B. Chap. P-35. An Act Respecting Provincial Parks. Cited as S.N.S. 1988, chap. 18.
C. Correspondence. 19 July 1994. R.G. MacGregor, Executive Director of Operations, Nova Scotia Department of Natural Resources.

Ontario (Province of)

A. Provincial Parks Act. Revised Statutes of Ontario 1990. Chap. P34
B. 'Provincial Park Regulations.' Regulation 952 of R.R.O. 1990 as amended by O. Reg. 32/91, 135/91, 383/91, 462/91, 144 /92, 174/92, 398/92, 587/ 92.
C. Tabloid: *Presqu'ile Provincial Park* (Summer 1995).
D. *Personal correspondence,* 13 June 1998.
E. *Guidelines for the Use of the Smokey Costume.* 1994. With a cover letter by Jeff Antoszek (fire technician). Ministry of Natural Resources.

Parks of the St Lawrence (Ontario)

A. Regulation 1023 of Revised Regulations of Ontario 1980. Made under the St Lawrence Parks Commission Act.
B. 'SK-2,' regulation made under the Liquor Licence Act – Possession of Liquor in parks managed or controlled by the St Clair Parkway Commission and the St Lawrence Parks Commission.
C. Correspondence. 16 Aug. 1994. Simon Wilson, Assistant to the Parks Coordinator, St Lawrence Parks Commission.

Yukon (Territory of)

A. Parks Act. Chap. 126.
B. 'Regulations in Respect of Yukon Government Campground.'
C. Correspondence. 19 July 1994. Jim McIntyre, Director, Parks and Outdoor recreation Branch, Yukon Renewable Resources.
D. Brochure: *Wilderness Traveller's 'No Trace Checklist.'*

BOOKS AND ARTICLES

Abrams, Philip. 1988. 'Notes on the Difficulty of Studying the State.' *Journal of Historical Sociology* 1(1): 58–89.

Beck, Ulrich. 1992. *Risk Society: Towards a New Modernity.* London: Sage.

– 1994. 'The Reinvention of Politics: Towards a Theory of Reflexive Modernization.' In *Reflexive Modernization.* Stanford: Stanford University Press.

Bell, V. 1993. 'Governing Childhood.' *Economy and Society* 33(22): 390–405.

Benjamin, Walter. 1979. *One Way Street.* London: NLB.

Berman, M. 1982. *All That Is Solid Melts into Air: The Experience of Modernity.* New York: Simon and Schuster.

Bourdieu, Pierre. 1992. *An Invitation to Reflexive Sociology.* Chicago: Chicago University Press.

Callon, Michel, and Bruno Latour. 1981. 'Unscrewing the Big Leviathan: How Actors Macro-Structure Reality and How Sociologists Help Them to Do So.' In *Advances in Social Theory and Methodology: Toward an Integration of Micro- and Macro-Sociologies,* ed. K. Knorr-Cetina and A.V. Cicourel. Boston: Routledge and Kegan Paul.

Carroll, Patrick. 1996. 'Science, Power, Bodies: The Mobilization of Nature as State Formation.' *Journal of Historical Sociology* 9 (June): 139–67.

Carson, Rachel. 1962. *Silent Spring.* Boston: Houghton Mifflin.

Castel, Robert. 1991. 'From Dangerousness to Risk.' In *The Foucault Effect: Studies in Governmentality,* ed. Graham Burchell, Colin Gordon, and Peter Miller. Chicago: University of Chicago Press.

Cosgrove, D.E. 1984. *Social Formation and Symbolic Landscape.* London: Croom Helm.

Cronon, William. 1995. *Uncommon Ground: Toward Reinventing Nature.* New York. W.W. Norton.

Davis, Mike. 1998. *The City of Quartz: Excavating the Future in Los Angeles.* London: Pimlico.

Dean, Mitchell. 1991. *The Constitution of Poverty.* London: Routledge.

Douglas, Mary. 1966. *Purity and Danger: An Analysis of Concepts of Pollution and Taboo.* London: Routledge and Kegan Paul.

Dwight F. Rettie. 1995. *Our National Park System.* Urbana: University of Illinois Press.

Eagleton, Terry. 1990. *The Ideology of the Aesthetic.* Oxford: Blackwell.

Ericson, Richard V., and Kevin D. Haggarty, 1997. *Policing the Risk Society.* Oxford: Clarendon Press.

Ewald, Francis. 1991. 'Insurance and Risk.' In *The Foucault Effect: Studies in Governmentality,* ed. Graham Burchell, Colin Gordon, and Peter Miller. Chicago: University of Chicago Press.

Everhart, William C. 1972. *The National Park Service.* New York: Praeger.

Foucault, Michel. 1972. 'On Geography.' In *Power/Knowledge: Selected Interviews and Other Writings 1972–1977*, ed. Colin Gordon. New York: Pantheon Books.

– 1975. *Discipline and Punish: The Birth of the Prison.* New York: Vintage Books.

– 1978. *The History of Sexuality.* Vol.1. Trans. Robert Hurley. New York: Random House.

– 1988. 'Technologies of the Self.' In *Technologies of the Self*, ed. Luther H. Martin et al. Amherst, Mass.: University of Massachusetts Press.

– 1991 [1979]. 'Governmentality.' In *The Foucault Effect: Studies In Governmentality*, ed. Graham Burchell, Colin Gordon, and Peter Miller. Chicago: University of Chicago Press.

Gilloch, Graeme. 1996. *Myth and Metropolis.* Cambridge: Polity Press.

Gordon, Colin. 1991. 'Governmental Rationality: An Introduction.' In *The Foucault Effect: Studies in Governmentality*, ed. Graham Burchell, Colin Gordon, and Peter Miller. Chicago: University of Chicago Press.

Grove, Richard E. 1990. 'Colonial Conservation, Ecological Hegemony and Popular Resistance: Towards a Global Synthesis.' In *Imperialism and the Natural World*, ed. John M. Mackenzie. Manchester: Manchester University Press.

Gregory, David. 1994. *Geographical Imaginations.* Oxford: Blackwell.

Gusfield, Joseph. 1963. *Symbolic Crusade: Status Politics and the American Temperance Movement.* Urbana: University of Illinois Press.

Hardin, Garrett. 1977. 'The Tragedy of the Commons.' In *Managing the Commons*, eds. Hardin, Garrett, and John Baden. San Francisco. W.H. Freeman.

Hart, H.L.A. 1961. *The Concept of Law.* Oxford: Clarendon Press.

Harvey, David. (1996). *Justice, Nature and the Geography of Difference.* Oxford: Blackwell.

Hawkins, Keith. 1984. *Environment and Enforcement.* Oxford: Clarendon Press.

Heidegger, Martin. 1964. 'The Question Concerning Technology.' In *Martin Heidegger: Basic Writings*, ed. David Krell. San Francisco: Harper.

Hermer, Joe, and Alan Hunt. 1996. 'Official Graffiti of the Everyday' *Law and Society Review* 30(3): 455–80.

Hunt, Alan. 1993. *Explorations in Law and Society.* New York: Routledge.

– 1997. *Governance of the Consuming Passions: A History of Sumptuary Regulation.* New York: St Martins Press.

Hunt, Alan, and Gary Wickham. 1994. *Foucault and Law: Towards a Sociology of Law as Governance.* London: Pluto Press.

Hutter, Bridget. 1997. *Compliance.* Oxford: Clarendon Press.

Ise, John. 1961. *Our National Park Policy: A Critical History.* Baltimore: John Hopkins University Press.

Ivins, W.M. 1973. *On the Rationalization of Sight.* Cambridge, Mass.: Harvard University Press.

Jacobs, Jane. 1961. *The Death and Life of Great American Cities.* New York: Vintage Books.

Kerouac, Jack. 1971 [1965]. *Desolation Angels.* New York: Bantam.

Killan, Gerald. 1993. *Protected Places: A History of Ontario's Provincial Park System.* Toronto: Dundurn Press.

Latour, Bruno. 1986. 'Visualization and Cognition: Thinking with Eyes and Hands.' In *Knowledge and Society: Studies in the Sociology of Culture Past and Present,* ed. H. Kuklick and E. Long. Greenwood, Conn.: JAI Press.

– 1987. *Science in Action: How to Follow Scientists and Engineers Through Society.* Milton Keynes, U.K.: Open University Press.

Law, John, and John Whittaker. 1988. 'On the Art of Representation: Notes on the Politics of Visualisation.' In *Picturing Power: Visual Depictions and Social Relations,* ed. Gordon Fyfe and John Law. London: Routledge.

Lefebvre, H. 1971 [1968]. *Everyday Life in the Modern World.* Trans. Sacha Rabinovitch. London: Penguin Press.

– 1991 [1974]. *The Production of Space.* Trans. Donald Nicholson-Smith. Oxford: Blackwell.

Leopold, Aldo. 1966. *A Sand County Almanac.* New York: Oxford University Press.

Lothian W.F. 1987. *A Brief History of Canada's National Parks.* Ottawa. Environment Canada Parks.

Lowry, William R. 1994. *The Capacity for Wonder: Preserving National Parks.* Washington: The Brookings Institute.

Markus, T.A. 1993. *Buildings and Power: Freedom and Social Control in the Origin of Modern Building Types.* New York: Routledge.

MacKenzie, John M. 1988. *The Empire of Nature: Hunting, Conservation and British Imperialism.* Manchester: Manchester University Press.

Maclean, Norman. 1976. *A River Runs Through It.* Chicago: University of Chicago Press.

Marty, Sid. 1984. *A Grand and Fabulous Notion: The First Century of Canada's Parks.* Ottawa: N.C. Press.

McGregor, Gaile. 1985. *The Wacousta Syndrome: Explorations in the Canadian Langscape.* Toronto: University of Toronto Press.

McLaughlin, Charles Capen. 1983. *The Papers of Frederick Law Olmstead.* Vol. 3. Baltimore: Johns Hopkins University Press.

McMullan, John L. 1998. 'The Arresting Eye: Discourse, Surveillance and Disciplinary Administration in Early Police Thinking.' *Social and Legal Studies* 7(1): 97–128.

Merchant, Carolyn. 1989. *The Death of Nature.* San Francisco: Harper.

Miles, John 1995. *Guardians of the Parks.* Taylor and Francis: Washington.

Miller, Peter, and Nikolas Rose. 1990. 'Governing Economic Life.' 19 (1) *Economy and Society,* 1–31.

Mitchell, Don. 1996. *The Lie of The Land: Migrant Workers and the California Landscape.* Minneapolis: University of Minnesota Press.

Mitchell, W. J. Thomas. 1994a. *Landscape and Power.* Chicago: University of Chicago Press.

– 1994b. *Picture Theory: Essays on Verbal and Visual Representation.* Chicago: University of Chicago Press.

Mitchell, Timothy. 1991. *Colonising Egypt.* Los Angeles: University of California Press.

Nash, Roderick. 1973. *Wilderness and the American Mind.* New Haven: Yale University Press.

Neumann, Roderick, P. 1996. 'Dukes, Earls, and Ersatz Edens: Aristocratic Nature Preservations in Colonial Africa.' *Society and Space* 14: 79–98.

Nowlan, Alden. 1982. 'The Bull Moose.' In *Canadian Poetry,* ed. Jack David and Robert Lecker. Vol. 2. Toronto: General Publishing.

Olmsted, Fredrick Law. 1852. *Walks and Talks of an American Farmer in England.* New York: Putnam.

– 1970 [1870]. *Public Parks and the Enlargement of Towns.* New York: Arno Press.

– 1983. *Creating Central Park, 1857–1861.* Vol. 3 of *The Papers of Frederick Law Olmsted,* ed. Charles E. Beveridge and David Schuyler. Baltimore: Johns Hopkins University Press.

Opie, Iona, and Peter Opie. 1974. *The Classic Fairy Tales.* New York: Oxford University Press:

O'Malley, Pat. 1991. 'Legal Networks and Domestic Security.' *Studies in Law, Politics and Society* 11: 171–90.

Pasquino, P. 1991. 'Theatrum Politicum: The Genealogy of Capital-Police and the State of Prosperity,' in G. Burchell. C. Gordon and P. Miller (eds.) *The Focault Effect: Studies in Governmentality.* London: Harvestor Wheatsheaf.

Paulus, I. 1974. *The Search for Pure Food: A Sociology of Legislation in Britain.* London: Robertson.

Pelt, Robert-Jan, 1994. 'A Site in Search of a Mission.' In *Anatomy of the Auschwitz Death Camp,* ed. Yisrael Gutman and Michael Berenbaum. Bloomington: Indiana University Press.

Pyne, Stephen J. 1982. *Fire In America: A Cultural History of Wildland and Rural Fire.* Princeton, NJ: Princeton University Press.

Reinarman, Craig. 1988. 'The Social Construction of an Alcohol Problem: The Case of Mothers Against Drunk Drivers and Social Control in the 1980s.' *Theory and Society* 17(1): 19–120.

Rettie, Dwight Fae. *Our National Park System: Caring for America's Greatest Natural and Historic Treasures.* Urbana: University of Illinois Press.

Rojek, Chris. 1992. '"The Eye of Power": Moral Regulation and the Professionalization of Leisure Management from the 1830s to the 1950s.' *Society and Leisure,* 15(1): 355–73.

Rose, Nikolas. 1990. *Governing the Soul: The Shaping of the Private Self.* London: Routledge.

– 1993. 'Government, Authority and Expertise in Advanced Liberalism.' *Economy & Society* 22(3): 283–99.

Runte, Alfred. 1987. *National Parks: The American Experience.* Lincoln: University of Nebraska Press.

– 1990. *Yosemite: The Embattled Wilderness.* Lincoln: University of Nebraska Press.

Said, Edward. 1993. *Culture and Imperialism.* London: Chatto and Windus.

Schama, Simon. 1995. *Landscape and Memory.* Toronto: Random House.

Sellars, Richard West. 1997. *Preserving Nature in the National Parks.* New Haven, Conn.: Yale University Press.

Sennett, R. 1970. *The Uses of Disorder: Personal Identity and City Life.* New York: Knopf.

Shields, Rob 1991. *Places on the Margin.* London: Routledge.

Short, John Rennie. 1991. *Imagined Country: Environment, Culture and Society.* London: Routledge.

Smith, Dorothy. 1990. *Texts, Facts and Femininity: Exploring the Relations of Ruling.* London: Routledge.

Smith, Neil. 1996. *The New Urban Frontier.* London: Routledge.

SPFE. 1924. *Journal for the Society of the Preservation of the Fauna of the Empire,* n.s., Pt. 4.

– 1928. *Journal for the Society of the Preservation of the Fauna of the Empire,* n.s. (June) pt. 8.

– 1930a. *Journal for the Society of the Preservation of the Fauna of the Empire,* n.s., pt 10. N.S. part XI.

– 1930b. *Journal for the Society of the Preservation of the Fuana of the Empire,* n.s., pt 10. N.S. part X.

– 1933. *Journal for the Society of the Preservation of the Fuana of the Empire,* n.s., Pt. 20.

Steinbeck, John. 1990 [1939]. *The Grapes of Wrath.* London: Mandarin Paperbacks.

Thévenot, L. 1984. 'Rules and Implements: Investment in Forms.' In *Social Science Information* 23(1): 1–45.

Thompson, E.P. 1990 [1975]. *Whigs and Hunters.* London: Penguin Books.

Turner, Louis, and John Ash. 1975. *The Golden Hordes: International Tourism and the Pleasure Periphery.* London: Constable.

Urry, John. 1990. *The Tourist Gaze: Leisure and Travel in Contemporary Societies.* London: Sage.

Valverde, Mariana. 1991. *The Age of Light, Soap and Water.* Toronto: McClelland & Stewart.

– 1994. 'Moral Capital.' *Canadian Journal of Law and Society* 9(1): 213–32.

– 1998. *Diseases of the Will: Alcohol and the Dilemmas of Freedom.* Cambridge: Cambridge University Press.

Van Loon, Joost, and Ida Sabelis. 1997. 'Recycling Time: The Temporal Complexity of Waste Management.' *Time and Society* 06(02): 287–307.

Walters, J.A. 1982. 'Social Limits to Tourism.' *Leisure Studies* 1(3): 295–304.

Williams, Raymond. 1973. *The Country and the City.* London: Chatto and Windus.

Wilson, Alexander. 1992. *The Culture of Nature.* Oxford: Blackwell.

Wylson, Anthony, and Patricia Wylson. 1994. *Theme Parks, Leisure Centres, Zoos and Aquaria.* Harlow, Essex: Longman.

Zukin, Sharon. 1991. *Landscapes of Power: From Detroit to Disney World.* Berkeley: University of California Press.

Index